T0254150

Designing for iOS with Sketch

Sian Morson

Apress®

Designing for iOS with Sketch

ISBN-13 (pbk): 978-1-4842-1459-6

ISBN-13 (electronic): 978-1-4842-1458-9

Managing Director: Welmoed Spahr
Lead Editor: Michelle Lowman
Technical Reviewer: Ashley Bennett, Gabriel Sebastien, and Scott Tolinski
Editorial Board: Steve Anglin, Louise Corrigan, James T. DeWolf, Jonathan Gennick, Robert Hutchinson, Michelle Lowman, James Markham, Susan McDermott, Matthew Moodie, Jeffrey Pepper, Douglas Pundick, Ben Renow-Clarke, Gwenan Spearing
Coordinating Editor: Mark Powers
Developmental Editor: Gary Schwartz
Copy Editor: Brendan Frost
Compositor: SPi Global
Indexer: SPi Global
Artist: SPi Global

Distributed to the book trade worldwide by Springer Science+Business Media New York, 233 Spring Street, 6th Floor, New York, NY 10013. Phone 1-800-SPRINGER, fax (201) 348-4505, e-mail orders-ny@springer-sbm.com, or visit www.springerOnline.com. Apress Media, LLC is a California LLC and the sole member (owner) is Springer Science + Business Media Finance Inc (SSBM Finance Inc). SSBM Finance Inc is a Delaware corporation.

For information on translations, please e-mail rights@apress.com, or visit www.apress.com.

Apress and friends of ED books may be purchased in bulk for academic, corporate, or promotional use. eBook versions and licenses are also available for most titles. For more information, reference our Special Bulk Sales–eBook Licensing web page at www.apress.com/bulk-sales.

Any source code or other supplementary material referenced by the author in this text is available to readers at www.apress.com/9781484214596. For detailed information about how to locate your book's source code, go to www.apress.com/source-code/. Readers can also access source code at SpringerLink in the Supplementary Material section for each chapter.

Dedicated to:
My nephew Shaddai—The future is yours.
and
My brother Khem—Stay strong.

Contents at a Glance

Contents

About the Author

Sian Morson is an entrepreneur, mobile enthusiast, and designer. In 2010, she founded Kollective Mobile, the Bay Area's premier mobile development agency.

Sian is also the CEO of Cast Beauty, a mobile e-commerce platform that provides users with personalized beauty recommendations based on their unique skin and hair profile—and the weather.

Sian lectures and speaks at conferences, universities, and symposia worldwide, including SXSW, ModevUX, and the University of Ohio. She also writes about mobile strategy, design, and entrepreneurship for a number of publications. Known as a mobile expert and thought leader, Sian has been featured and quoted in *Forbes*, *The Wall Street Journal, Inc.*, *Black Enterprise*, *Ebony*, *NPR*, and *AdAge*.

A tireless advocate for equality and diversity in technology, Sian has a keen interest in bridging the digital divide. To this end, she volunteers her time with various nonprofits working to bring equality to tech.

Sian has been named one of the top women in tech to follow on Twitter by the Huffington Post, Craig Newmark, and CEO World Magazine. In 2014, Sian was invited to the White House as a part of the 2nd Annual LGBTW Tech & Innovation Summit and awarded L'Oreal USA's Next Generation Award in 2015.

An internationally exhibited artist, Sian enjoys fusing her creativity with technology. Her video artwork has featured in the prestigious Optica Festival in Spain, Director's Lounge Berlin, Aakriti Gallery in Mumbai, India, and MoCADA Museum in Brooklyn, NY.

About the Technical Reviewers

Ashley Bennett is a senior designer at New Media Campaigns where she leads the web and app design process for nonprofits, businesses, and universities. In addition to using Sketch in her daily work, she blogs about a variety of Sketch topics for her company blog and Smashing Magazine. She currently resides in Charlotte, NC with her husband and two dogs.

Sebastien Gabriel is a senior designer at Google, focusing on Google Chrome.

Scott Tolinski is the creator of Level Up Tutorials and a Senior Web Developer for Team Detroit. In addition to publishing over 700 popular web development and design tutorials with Level Up Tutorials, Scott has also worked on the global redesign of Ford.com. He can be reached via Twitter at @stolinski or @leveluptuts.

Acknowledgments

To everyone who worked on this book, thank you. Especially my Technical Reviewers: Sebastien, Ashley, and Scott. Thank you for making this book better. Your feedback was invaluable!

Also, many thanks to Michelle, Mark, and Welmoed!

Why Sketch?

Congratulations! You've made the decision to start using Sketch to design for iOS. This is a big decision. You may or may not be aware of the controversy currently brewing in the design community. What controversy you ask? The one of whether to use what has been the industry standard for years, Adobe Photoshop, or a new, smaller, and faster alternative called Sketch.

Lately, many designers have opted for Sketch, which was once a little-known graphics software program by Bohemian Coding, a Dutch software development firm from The Hague. Many have incorporated the app into their design workflow. These designers include Khoi Vihn, the internationally known graphic designer and former Design Director of the *New York Times*, design consultancies, and companies such as BuzzFeed, SEGA, and Google, plus startups like Pinterest and Groupon. Sketch seems to be taking the design world by storm. The app, which is available for Mac OS only, is less expensive at $99, faster, and smaller in size (about 40MB) than Photoshop. Add to this the fact that it was specifically created for designers working in UI design for mobile apps and the Web in mind, and you have a compelling argument for Sketch.

This book is not about convincing you to use Sketch over Photoshop. Since you are reading this, I am making the assumption that you have already made a decision to explore how Sketch can be incorporated into your design workflow. And to be fair, Photoshop has its uses. You will still need to use it, as its name implies, to edit photos and raster files and other tasks. Photoshop has been the de facto "go-to" software program for graphic designers for decades because there are some things that it does better than any other software on the market.

This book's primary purpose is to introduce you to Sketch and why it is a great program for anyone considering interface design for iOS devices. I will, in places, point out areas where Sketch and Photshop differ, but what I don't want to do is to say that Photoshop is bad and Sketch is good. Any search on Sketch vs. Photosop will yield plenty of articles on why designers feel that one program is better than the other. Some of those points will be repeated here, but only as they pertain to the overall purpose of the book; that is, designing great interfaces for iOS.

A Bit of History

While Photoshop has been on the market for approximately 25 years—its initial release was in February of 1990—Sketch is relatively new on the design scene. Its initial versions failed to make a huge ripple in the design community. While some designers took notice, at the outset it was not adopted as widely as compared to today. Adobe's suite of design software, previously known as Creative Suite, was still the industry standard. Indeed, many designers and agencies still swear by it.

Then, in 2013, in a move that proved to be a shift for their business, Adobe announced that its Creative Suite would only be available via a cloud-based subscription plan. The old DVD versions would no longer be offered, and users would need to sign up for a $40 monthly subscription plan to use the software. Creative Suite included some of Adobe's top programs used by design professionals worldwide—Photoshop, InDesign, Premiere Pro, AfterEffects, Dreamweaver, Illustrator, and other Adobe products would now be moving to the cloud. The product was renamed Adobe Creative Cloud.

To be clear, users would see no clear difference while using the software via Creative Cloud, and it still needed to be downloaded and installed on their machines. The main difference with the cloud-based model was that every so often (usually every 30 days or so) an Internet connection would be required to ensure that the version of the software is valid. If the validation check against Adobe's servers found that the subscription is no longer valid, then the software would be deemed invalid and could no longer be used.

The new subscription model offered varying price points—one for students at $19.99 a month and regular pricing for $49.99. Considering that a full version of the Adobe Creative Suite could run in the $2,500 range, some saw this as a good deal. But there were some in the designer community that found the change to be disruptive. Today, Creative Cloud allows access to the entire stack of Adobe's suite of programs, and many designers have signed onto the new service. Recent reports show that Adobe now has 4.61 million paying Creative Cloud customers, and it is looking to increase that to 6 million by the end of 2015.

The latest update to Creative Cloud will be artboards in Photoshop (a key Sketch feature that we will discuss later). Notably, it also includes Adobe Design Space, a new HTML-based design tool with a scaled-down interface that appears remarkably Sketch-like.

Photoshop has long maintained its position as the de facto standard for graphic designers creating interfaces for the Web and mobile applications. For years, it stood unchallenged, but privately, many designers were fed up with Photoshop's and Illustrator's bloat. The programs were huge and required significant RAM resources to run. Photoshop alone requires at least 2GB of RAM with 8GB recommended.

Some designers, this one included, felt that with the changes taking place on the Web, and with the growing popularity of mobile phones and tablets, Adobe wasn't doing the best job of keeping Photoshop up to date, and that it was trying to do too much and to be too many things to too many people. Its rendering style wasn't very efficient, and anyone who has ever created a Photoshop file was aware of the program's propensity for creating HUGE files in the program's proprietary format (PSD). UI designers had special needs and many felt that those needs were not being met.

Still, the ability for any newcomer to challenge Adobe's dominance in the design space remained virtually impossible for quite some time. Companies invested in Creative Suite for their teams, and designers dealt with their frustrations hoping for better options to come.

Enter Sketch 2

Sketch first made its way onto my radar in late 2013, well before its current iteration (v3.3.3). Version 2 was already out, and some friends of mine were discussing the program. I took a look at the interface and thought that it seemed very simple. Maybe too simple, as shown in Figure 1-1. At that time, I was still a fan of Fireworks for interface design, mostly because it offered very focused tools and wasn't as overwhelming as Photoshop. At the time, I didn't care enough to dive deeper or to get a better understanding of what Bohemian Coding was trying to accomplish with Sketch.

Figure 1-1. The Sketch 2 interface

However, like the little engine that could, the scrappy software studio made steady and consistent improvements to the program. From the beginning, they have been listening and paying close attention to the feedback from designers in their growing community. This is apparent in every Sketch release.

First off, it's important to note that Sketch is a Mac OS X app. This means that Sketch was created initially to run solely and exclusively on the Mac operating system. As such, releases were timed and optimized to work with various releases of the OS by Apple. Starting with Sketch version 2.3, it was known as the "Snow Leopard" release. The team added features such as Boolean operations, background blur, and the ability to import PDF and EPS files into designs.

The developers also focused on improving the program's responsiveness and speed. Features like background blur were important for iOS designers, as this feature was prominent in Apple's revamp of iOS. With the new look being prominently displayed on iPhones everywhere, the Sketch development team had the foresight to add this feature to the program. This is the kind of thinking that made designers take notice of Sketch.

Sketch Mirror

Another feature for which Bohemian Coding showed a lot of foresight was the addition of Sketch Mirror (see Figure 1-2). This handy feature allowed designers to preview their work in all its glory on their iPhones or iPad. Distributed as a standalone iPhone app and available via the App Store, Sketch Mirror scales your designs up or down depending on resolution, and it allowed you to preview your designs directly on an iPhone or iPad. This small change demonstrated Bohemian Coding's commitment, not only to designers working on mobile apps, but to iOS itself; that is, Sketch gave a nod to the dominant mobile platform at the time.

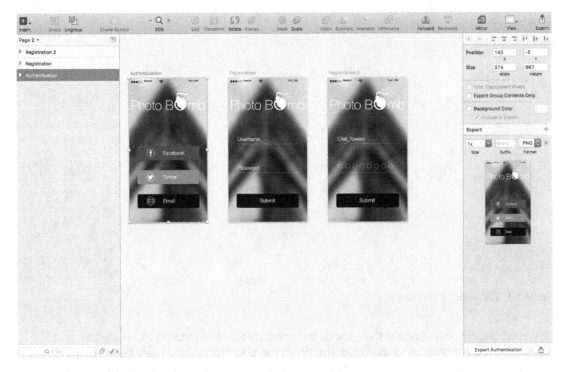

Figure 1-2. Sketch Mirror allows designers to preview designs on an iPhone

Not satisfied to sit back on their laurels, the team at Bohemian Coding kept improving the program. Sketch 2.4 brought enhancements to masking, greatly improved speed when grouping, resizing, moving, and ungrouping large amounts of layers, multiple bug fixes, as well as improved color accuracy, something that is of critical importance to all designers.

Bye, Bye Fontcase . . .

A critical move that proved that Bohemian Coding had the needs and desires of designers everywhere at heart was the retiring of Fontcase. For those who are unaware, Fontcase was a font management system that allowed designers and graphic designers to store, manage, and preview their fonts. While this might sound superfluous and unnecessary, for designers, something like Font Manager is incredibly important. Designers need to know which apps are installed on their system and what they look like, and Font Manager makes it very easy to browse for fonts. The program was built directly into iOS for a while. Citing issues with font activation in Fontcase and sandboxing, the team at Bohemian Coding wisely made the decision to retire Fontcase. Apparently, there were major issues, and Fontcase wasn't working properly. Moreover, designers were having a hard time understanding just why it was needed in the first place. From the Bohemian Coding blog:

> *"We've come to the realization that Fontcase's main features are just not needed or appropriate in this day and age, and the time has come to retire it. Therefore, we've made the difficult decision to remove the app from the store. We will offer non-sandboxed copies to anyone who's experiencing problems, but this will be the last Fontcase release."*

With Fontcase out of the way, the team continued to perfect the program. Minor releases followed after that, which showed that the team was paying attention to goings-on in the design world while working diligently to address the bugs in the software. It is important to note as well that releases, fixes, and updates of Sketch were timelier than those in Photoshop. Designers often bemoaned the fact that major updates and releases of Photoshop were spaced roughly two years apart. Sketch, on the other hand, shipped updates and releases at a clip of about every month or so. This speaks volumes about the advantages of having a leaner and more agile development team.

So, Sketch had gotten the attention of the design community. Nevertheless, only the more daring designers would ditch Photoshop and make a complete transition to Sketch. Many others were watching and waiting to see how the software would evolve and whether it would become a true contender.

Apple Design Award

Every year since 1996, Apple announces the winner of its prestigious Design Awards at its annual Worldwide Developers Conference (WWDC). The Design Awards are distributed to best-in-class apps that exhibit the best in design and development. It is a high honor that Apple bestows on developers who have achieved the highest standards in design using the company's software products. These are the apps that set the standard for the user experience that Apple expects on its platform. They are altogether innovative and inspiring. When selecting apps for the Apple Design Awards, Apple looks for apps that are: delightful, innovative, state of the art, engaging, enabling, and well designed. The awards celebrate what the company believes to be the best apps created by independent developers from all over the world.

Sketch was among the Design Award winners in 2012. For designers who are attracted to Apple's software and hardware products because of their high standard of design, this was a pretty big deal. It meant not only that Sketch's developers had gotten the attention of the design community for creating an app that would make their collective lives easier, but also that they had done so while creating a beautiful app. Typically, software's functionality often overshadows what it looks like and how it *feels* to use it. By winning the prestigious Design Award from Apple, Bohemian Coding had firmly established itself as a leading design and software development company. Moreover, with design becoming more of a focus for many companies, Sketch was the one to watch.

Sketch 3

By 2014, the team at Bohemian Coding had been working on Sketch for over two years and had increased from a paltry two members handling development and design to about five. They had also learned the value of outsourcing and used third-party developers to help to create a brand new Sketch website and a helpful video highlighting all of the latest features.

However, it wasn't until the release of Sketch 3.0 in April that more people in the design community began to take notice. Two years after the release of Sketch 2.0, Sketch 3.0 arrived. The company had a new expanded team and a suite of new and improved features. As mentioned, adding team members and outsourcing some key elements helped the team to focus on just the product. They rebooted, redesigned their website, and listened to the very vocal designer community who were interested in seeing changes and updates, particularly in symbols, exporting, and the fledgling inspector feature.

By this time, mobile apps were well on their way to leading the world, and designers were heavily embracing mobile paradigms that weren't just device specific. The Web was quickly becoming mobile-first as well. Designers wanted and needed software whose developers understood that design was changing as a discipline. They'd been using Photoshop for years, and it seemed that Adobe wasn't listening to the complaints of the designer community.

When Sketch 3 was released, Bohemian Coding offered it as a free upgrade to those who'd purchased and owned Sketch 2. For one week in April, Sketch 3 was available in the Mac OS App Store for $49.99. This is when I first bought my own copy. After April 21, 2014, the app's price increased to $79.99 and then later to its current price of $99.99. Based on its price alone, Sketch has a huge advantage over the incredibly expensive Adobe Photoshop, Illustrator, or Creative Cloud. At $49.99 a month, this comes out to roughly $600 a year. Given its robust feature set, Sketch is a bargain considering the power it packs. Those who still aren't sold on the software can download a free 30-day trial version.

After Sketch 3 was released to the designer community, more frequent updates followed. Each subsequent update raised the bar in terms of performance improvements, new features, and bug fixes. As of this writing, the latest version of Sketch is Version 3.3.3. The Bohemian Coding team not only seems to be listening to the needs to designers and taking their needs into account, they also seem to be following one of the most notable startup edicts—listen and pay close attention to your customers, and iterate your product quickly.

With a growing community of designers providing quality feedback, the team at Bohemian Coding made multiple changes and improvements to the program. They focused on making Sketch the dream "designer toolbox," with everything a designer needs to make great websites and apps right at their fingertips.

To be fair, it is important to point out that Sketch isn't for everyone or every design. If you're working with bitmaps in particular, then you likely won't find a better editor than Photoshop. However, many designers have found that once they pick up Sketch, they can do most things that relate to UI design easily with it.

In addition to the amazing improvements being made to the program, the developer community began to rally around the app, and a vibrant community of plug-ins was created to supplement what the app could not do. Bohemian Coding encouraged this third-party development and understood this as a way to build support in the development community. With the line between coding and design quickly being blurred, it was important to get developers on board as well. I cover some of the more helpful plug-ins later in this book.

The Sketch 3 Interface

The Sketch 3 interface is intentionally simple, minimalistic, and streamlined, as you can see in Figure 1-3. There is a toolbar across the top that allows for easy customization, and users can add or remove tools from this toolbar according to their personal preferences.

Figure 1-3. The Sketch 3 interface

The layers list on the left lets you name and find the layers on your design.

The right side of the screen features the inspector, which offers you the tools to change the properties of items currently displayed on the screen. Every item on the screen can be changed or altered using the inspector.

As you can see in Figure 1-4, compared to Photoshop with its massive list of tools and many windows, Sketch is barely there. Even after I became more comfortable with Photoshop, I was always daunted by the sheer number of features and tools it offered—some of which I've never used. With Sketch, virtually every feature will come in handy at some point. I find the interface to be welcoming. It's bright, light, and not at all overwhelming—especially for a beginner. But don't let the simplicity of the interface fool you. The simplicity is by design. Sketch is powerful graphic design software that allows you to create beautiful designs.

Figure 1-4. Adobe Photoshop 6 interface

Raster vs. Vector

You might be asking yourself, "So, aside from price and the user interface, how exactly does Sketch differ from Photoshop?" It's important to know and understand the differences between the two. To be clear, there are some things that Photoshop can do that Sketch simply cannot and it wasn't meant to do them. Where Sketch really shines is in interface design. In fact, it seems to be have been built specifically for this purpose. As such, it allows UI designers a greater feature set that is tailor-made for their needs.

One of the main differences, however, is that Sketch is a vector-based tool and Photoshop is not. Photoshop is a photoediting tool and was not intended as an optimal Web or mobile

UI design tool. As mentioned in my last book, (*Learn Design for iOS Development*, Apress, 2014) Fireworks came the closest as a reasonable alternative for UI design. But the app failed to catch on and, as a result, Adobe stopped supporting it in 2013.

Arguably, in Photoshop, the percentage of its features that are really useful for UI design is estimated to be roughly 20 percent. This means that designers were downloading and using a program of almost 1GB the last time I checked in which 80 percent of the features were not useful to them or even created with them in mind. Indeed, Photoshop as its name implies, was intended to be a tool for the editing and manipulation of photos. Hence, it is raster-based, meaning that each image is made up of pixels that are then arranged to display an image.

One great thing about raster images is that they can display lots of colors and allow editors to get beautiful lighting and shading effects using the raster format. Unfortunately, they can't be displayed larger than they are without losing some quality. As such, they yield pretty huge files. Try blowing up a raster image, and you'll lose quality fast. Zooming in will reveal each individual pixel that makes up the image. Designers have understood for years that Photshop was initially developed as a raster-editing tool. Indeed, Photoshop was created by some amateur photographers and programmers for the purpose of displaying their photography. Some would say that a more worthy comparison would be between Fireworks and Sketch. However, this became a moot point when Adobe stopped supporting Fireworks in 2013. The program is still being offered as a part of Creative Cloud, but Adobe has no plans to continue offering fixes for the program.

Sketch is a 100-percent vector-based tool. A *vector* is made up of points, lines, curves, and, most importantly, math. In Chapter 3, we'll see how Sketch allows designers to edit numerical values to change the way a shape appears on the screen. When viewing raster and vector images with the naked eye, they may look the same. But zooming in, you will see that, as mentioned previously, a raster image, because it is made up of pixels, loses its quality the further you enlarge it. Curves in particular will appear blurred on raster images. Zooming in on a vector image yields a different view. Regardless of how much you zoom in, a vector image will maintain its quality and will remain crisp and clear regardless of size on a curve.

Why is this important? Because more and more, designers are being asked to design for a variety of screen sizes and resolutions, especially when it comes to mobile devices. With vectors created in Sketch, you save yourself the hassle of designing at @2× as you would in Photoshop to accommodate the growing number of screen sizes and resolutions now available on the market. Also, Sketch allows you to design in pixels, which is what most interfaces are measured in these days.

Figure 1-5 shows the difference when zoomed in on how raster and vector images appear. This has huge ramifications for designers who must designs across platforms and for Retina screens, which are quickly becoming the norm in mobile displays, particularly for iOS.

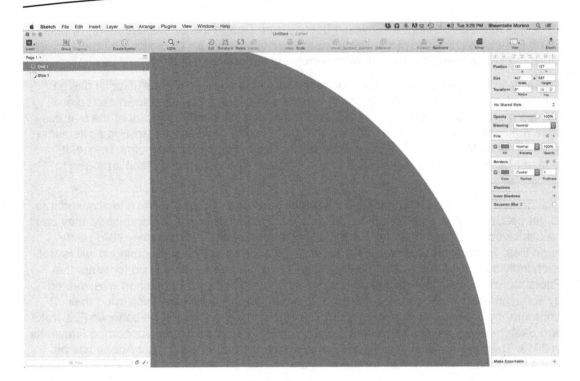

Figure 1-5. A vector shape viewed at 400 percent in Sketch 3

Note in Figure 1-5 the smoothness of the curve of the circle shape created in Sketch. When not zoomed in, vectors and rasters look more or less the same, and it may be hard to tell them apart. Once you zoom in, however, you will see that the curve of the circle that is a vector will be razor sharp.

In graphics, vector shapes are created using Bezier curves. Typically, vector shapes have two points that are controlled by handles. Each point allows the user to manipulate the curve. The final result is drawn based on the positions of the points. We will discuss Bezier curves in Chapter 3 when we move onto shapes, but this is the gist of working with vectors and how they maintain their sharpness. Vectors can be scaled to any size regardless of how much you zoom in or how large the image becomes. This is critical for designers, and it has become one of the flagship features of Sketch.

Figure 1-6 shows a circle shape created in Adobe Photoshop. Note the jagged, rounded edges of the circle. The raster is made up of pixels, and once zoomed in, or if the image size is increased, you will see that pixelation is especially evident at the circle's border.

Figure 1-6. A raster shape viewed at 200 percent in Adobe Photoshop

Because Sketch is vector graphic tool, any shapes created within the application will retain their quality when scaling.

As a designer, it is important to have options, and having access to a tool created specifically with designers in mind is essential. Also, it is important to note that using Sketch does not bar one from continuing to use Photshop and Creative Cloud. It is entirely possible to use both, and I believe that some designers, in fact, do use both. What Sketch brings to the table for designers is a new level of flexibility and a more refined workflow. If, as a designer, your focus is on user interface or icon design, then you must consider that for some, the cost of Adobe Creative cloud can be prohibitive.

The vast majority of designers have long opted for Macs over PCs for work, and indeed Apple's focus on design and creativity has been touted for years. Johnny Ive is a modern-day hero for creative designers worldwide. His partnership with Steve Jobs led to the creation of some of the most iconic products that the world had ever seen. Among them, the candy-colored iMac, sleek white MacBooks, and eventually the iPhone and iPad. Designers have idolized Ive for years, and since Steve Jobs' passing, Ive has helped to keep the company at the forefront of design. Sketch caters specifically to designers, and its price point made it immediately attractive for those who were interested in giving it a try. Its close alignment with Apple made it easy for designers to explore the new tool.

A major feature of Sketch 3 is its speed. Coming in at only 32MB, the program is fast, as it takes up less processing power on newer, Intel-based Macs with Retina screens. Version 3 was also rebuilt especially for Macs and optimized for OS X and it responds well to users' needs. It allows designers to create and view an entire project using its artboard system and still maintain a relatively small footprint. Anyone using Photoshop is aware that PSDs can run well into multiple-gigabyte sizes for complex projects with lots of screens.

By being built exclusively for Mac OS X, it allows the program to adapt some features for free. For example, I mentioned the removal of Fontcase previously. Sketch now is able to use Mac OS's built-in font rendering engine. Add auto-save to that, and you've got an enviable combination. A direct download from the Mac OS App Store doesn't hurt either.

Community

Another major benefit of Sketch is that it listens to a large community which often drives program updates. There are Twitter lists, Facebook groups, and even a curated list of articles on Medium, the online blogging platform (see Figure 1-7). Releases address a combination of concerns that are important to community members, as well as issues that are important to the developers, which build on the solid base that they have created with the program.

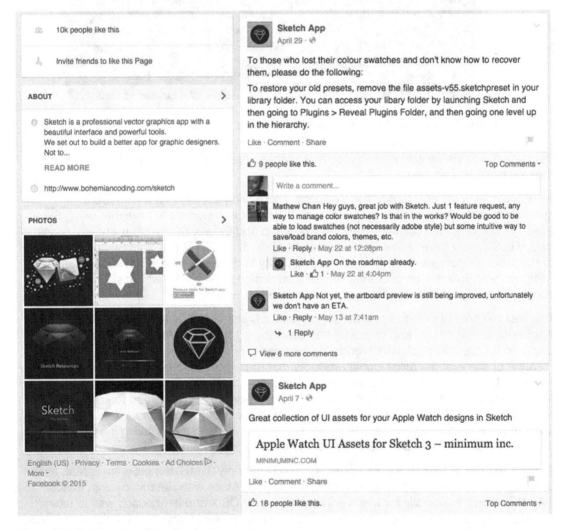

Figure 1-7. Sketch community on Facebook

The Bohemian Coding website proudly lists other apps that integrate with Sketch, groups and sites that focus on the program, as well as resources for anyone wanting to learn the program. They also offer a subscription-based newsletter that directly addresses questions from the community, offers help on common issues, and features plug-ins to help users with their workflow. All in all, the Sketch community is fairly resourceful. In addition to the free resources, there are paid courses on Udemy and even a Sketch class on TreeHouse taught by Sketch designer Christopher Downer.

Meng To created one of the most popular of these independent courses. Meng is a designer and a strong proponent of the growing school of thought that designers should also code. He wrote *Design & Code*, which is an electronic book that teaches designers the finer points of designing for iOS with some basic coding using Xcode. In it, he raves about the ease of using Sketch and an online prototyping tool called Flinto for making easy prototypes. Meng now travels the world offering live classes that teach designers how to design apps using Sketch and build them using Swift, Apple's new development language. *Design & Code* prompted me to take another, closer look at Sketch—and I'm glad that I did.

I've always found Photoshop's UI to be daunting. The sheer number of tools available was a barrier to me even wanting to learn how to use it. I've heard similar stories from some first-time designers. Sketch has a pared-down interface, and it is more similar to Fireworks, another Adobe tool. I liked Fireworks because it seemed to be created, like Sketch, with designers in mind; specifically, designers who were more focused on user interface design for the Web and mobile apps. When I opened Sketch for the first time, I immediately felt comfortable. I was able to customize the toolbar to include those tools that I would use most often. It allowed me to spend more time designing with fewer distractions, which led me to try to out the specific tools that I needed.

Photoshop isn't the only comparison to make. Surely there are other design tools on the market. There are other niche graphics programs on the market that could appeal to designers who are looking for an alternative to Photoshop. Apps like Skala come to mind as worthy alternatives for designers who are looking for something different and built with them in mind.

Effects are another reason that designers will appreciate Sketch. Moreover, being able to add more than one effect to a layer at a time is a great addition to the feature set of Sketch. This includes blurs, reflections, borders, and inner and outer shadows.

Exporting with Sketch is as easy as making a few selections and clicking a few buttons. It is possible to export an entire artboard at multiple resolutions. You will appreciate this feature if you've tried to export your designs in other programs.

iOS9

iOS9 is the latest version of the iPhone operating system. Much has been said of the "under-the-hood" changes that have been made, while some have claimed that they changes are largely minor. Nevertheless, though iOS9 offers optimizations that may not be apparent to the eye, it is still a significant update.

You might recall that in 2013, Apple overhauled the user interface of iOS, changing the look for the first time since the original iPhone release in 2007. iOS7 introduced an entirely different look and feel to iPhone and iPad users. It moved away from skeuomorphism and towards the trend of flat design. It also introduced new tools like the Control Center, a panel that rises with a swipe from the bottom of the screen to reveal a frosted panel offering easy access to airplane mode, Bluetooth, and other options. The new OS also introduced a brand-new "Flat Design" language for Apple. Designers had to get on board, and they did. Indeed new apps featured an iOS7-specific look and feel.

iOS8 further refined the UI with the addition of frameworks like HealthKit and HomeKit. But neither of these represented huge shifts in the design language or presented major issues for designers.

Released in the fall of 2015, iOS9 will be the latest iteration of the operating system for mobile devices by Apple. So, you might be asking yourself what to expect and how to manage these changes while designing using Sketch. The good news is that from a design standpoint, there haven't been many changes that designers need to worry about. iOS9, at its core, offers more stability and fixes to the mobile device operating system and more changes to iOS's core stable of applications. The changes will offer users a more a consistent experience across devices, bug fixes, a considerable boost in performance, and, most notably, a significant reduction in the size of the OS. Users can expect new features like multitasking, a new keyboard, new apps like Apple News, and the addition of public transit information to Apple Maps.

While the changes aren't significant from a design standpoint, there are a few features of which designers will need to be aware; not only will these features change how users interact with not only their devices, but they could also affect interaction with apps.

App Switcher

Switching between apps is still possible by double-clicking the Home button; however, doing so will now reveal a newer vertical view of all of the programs currently open. Users are able to swipe through as before.

New Navigation for Photos

Now when going through photos in your Camera Roll, you can simply swipe along a list of photos to view one in greater detail. You no longer have to tap each photo individually.

New Back Button

The addition of a Back button that allows users to go back to a previous program marks a new navigational element in iOS9. The button allows users to navigate back to a previous program without hitting the Home button.

New System Font: San Francisco

The system font for iOS has been updated. Some of you might remember that iOS made heavy use of Helvetica as its official system font. This has been updated to a custom font Apple calls San Francisco. Those with a keen eye will notice a subtle difference between the two fonts, but most will agree that it is not significant (see Figure 1-8). There has been some debate in the design community as to whether San Francisco is more "readable." Apple sure thinks so.

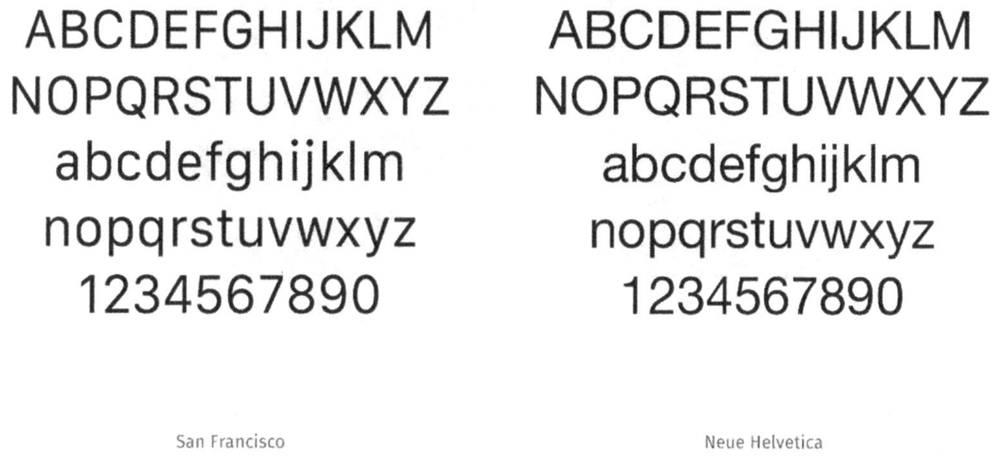

ABCDEFGHIJKLM
NOPQRSTUVWXYZ
abcdefghijklm
nopqrstuvwxyz
1234567890

ABCDEFGHIJKLM
NOPQRSTUVWXYZ
abcdefghijklm
nopqrstuvwxyz
1234567890

San Francisco   Neue Helvetica

Figure 1-8. San Francisco and Helvetica Neue fonts

San Francisco is from the San Serif family tree, and it consists of two different fonts: the SF and the SF Compace fonts. The SF font ships on iOS and OS X, and SF Compact ships with the Apple Watch. The two are related, but there are slight differences in the round states and slightly more space between letters to improve readability in the San Francisco font. The font also covers a variety of languages like Greek, Vietnamese, and Polish. The typeface was created by the Apple team.

The Apple Watch

While WWDC is typically when new operating systems are announced, during a special September event in 2014, Apple announced a new product—the Apple Watch. Naturally, this had the designer world buzzing. It also presented a new design challenge for those who work on iOS. Surely the new watch would run on a version of iOS, and it did.

To date, quite a few Apple Watch apps have made it into the Apple App store since its official launch in April 2015. Some major retailers, including Target, Starbucks, eBay, and Nike have released Apple Watch apps in the store and some not-so-major ones have as well.

The Apple Watch arrived with a fair amount of excitement from pretty much everyone working in tech. Apple was making a long-rumored venture into the world of wearables, and with their penchant for design, the world was waiting to see not only what the watch looked like but how it would work and what challenges, if any, it would present for designers.

As shown in Figure 1-9, the Apple Watch comes in two sizes; 38mm and 42mm (measured by height). Thus the screens are roughly 340px by 272px for the 38mm version and 390px by 312px for the 42mm version.

Figure 1-9. The Apple Watch comes in two sizes, 38mm and 42mm

Both Apple Watch sizes show the same content and use Dynamic Type to make sure that items shift to fit in the available space.

As with every other Apple product, the Apple watch has its own Human Interface Guidelines. If you're interested in designing for the Apple Watch, you should study and read these guidelines. The Apple Watch has very specific design principles when it comes to typography, color, customization, icons, and animation.

The Apple Watch runs on its own software called watchOS. Now in version 2, it is a modified version of iOS, and it runs only on the Apple Watch.

I won't go into specifics on designing for the Apple Watch in this book, but suffice it to say that the watch presents not only a new frontier, but new challenges for designers. And, as usual, there are Sketch Apple Watch templates available for your download and use.

Other changes to iOS9 include new apps, like News, and new features and improvements to the Maps and Notes apps. While there may not be any specific changes to the overall design language of the operating system in iOS9, it is important to note some of these apps, especially the new ones, offer a new way of presenting information. In them, you can find clues as to where Apple is going with their design language. Designers who are new to designing for iOS are encouraged to peruse these new apps to understand best design practices for their products. For example, if you're just starting out and you are curious about the best way to implement a segmented control, aside from the Human Interface Guidelines, Apple's built-in apps are the best way to learn how to be a great iOS designer (see Figure 1-10).

Figure 1-10. Old and new built-in apps in iOS9

> **Tip**   Currently, Apple's built-in apps now number 29. In addition to these, there are an additional 11 apps that users can download from Apple.

Summary

While Sketch was originally created for the Mac and OSX, Sketch and iOS make a great combination for designers interested in creating apps. With Sketch, designers who design for iOS, watchOS, and even MacOS now have a tool specifically developed for them. The makers of Sketch have said repeatedly that they have no intention of producing a Windows version of the program. This means that the program will continue to evolve with Mac users in mind. Designing for iOS with Sketch makes sense for anyone willing to take the time to learn the program and dive into properly designing apps for iPhones and iPads. Learning Sketch is a great first step.

In the next chapter, we walk you through installing Sketch and introduce you to the interface and other features that you will need to know as you begin your journey of designing for iOS with Sketch.

Chapter 2

Getting Started with Sketch

The latest version of Sketch is Sketch 3 (version 3.3.3 to be exact), and this book assumes that you are running this version. If you have an older version, you will need to update it. As mentioned, Sketch is a Mac-only application, and it requires OS X (Mavericks) or later to run. If you are running an older version of Mac OS X, you will also need to update that.

Installation

To install Sketch, you must download it from the Bohemian Coding site directly. On December 1, Sketch announced that it was pulling the app from the Mac OS store. Citing issues with delays in timely approvals of updates and technical limitations imposed by the App Store guidelines, in a post on their website, Bohemian Coding outlined to users how they could continue to enjoy Sketch and what the changes would mean. Mostly the Sketch community was behind the decision as it likely means quicker updates and more improvements to the program. The program will take you through the registration process by asking for your license key. Sketch costs $99.00.

Figure 2-1. *You can purchase Sketch 3 directly from the Bohemian Coding site*

To install the app that you purchased from Bohemian Coding, download it and move the program from the Downloads folder to the Applications folder. You can also just double-click the downloaded .DMG file and follow the directions. Either way, the file must be added to your Applications folder.

Once it's there, you can then double-click to start the program. That should be it! You've now installed the exciting new design program Sketch, and you are ready to learn more about designing for iOS!

Opening Sketch

Once you open the program, you will see that the Sketch interface is fairly simple. It was created to be as streamlined and as minimalistic as possible in order to allow you to focus completely on your work. There are no floating panels, and everything you need is easily accessible from the three main areas within the interface. These areas are as follows:

1. The toolbar along the top

2. The Layer panel on the left

3. The Inspector panel on the right

4. The canvas in the center of the screen where your actual design work
    will take place

Sketch offers infinite scrolling. This gives you a great deal of control over what you see on screen. With this feature, you can scroll infinitely in any direction and add as much content as you'd like to your canvas, which is shown in Figure 2-2.

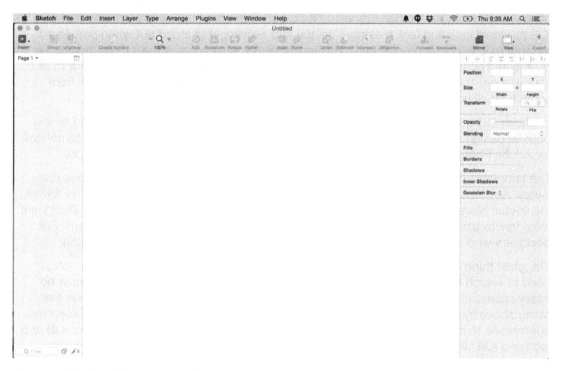

Figure 2-2. The Sketch interface in version 3.3.3

Tip   If you scroll to the far left, right, or anywhere on your canvas and lose your place, you can always return to your design by using the shortcut ⌘1 or by going to the View menu and selecting Center Canvas.

The Canvas

The middle area of the screen is called the *canvas*. This is where you will spend your time, as your design will actually live in this space. Adjustments that you make in the Inspector will manifest themselves in your canvas area.

When you are beginning your design, you must have the correct dimensions for the iPhone handy. As you know, the iOS UI design consists of many unique elements, each with Apple's own unique touch. These elements are an integral part of the iOS design language. You may have already installed the San Francisco font, but what about the other elements that give iOS its iconic look and feel, making it unique and allowing it to stand out when compared to other mobile operating systems? This includes elements such as the iOS keyboard, the segmented controls, and the Control Center that effortlessly slides up from the bottom of your iPhone. You may ask yourself, do we we need to design all of these elements from scratch? Well no, of course.

In March 2014, it was announced that Sketch would ship with an iOS8 GUI created by the popular design studio Teehan+Lax. The Sketch team had previously released iOS templates for Adobe Photoshop, so the designers were already familiar with their detailed work.

The template contains an exquisitely detailed, layered file containing multiple shapes and layers. All of these shapes and layers were painstakingly recreated in Sketch's native format, the vector. More exciting was the fact that these shapes and layers were editable. Designers were free to use them to create new designs, providing they followed Sketch's terms. For designers who were interested in designing for iOS using Sketch, this was a blessing.

The great thing about the GUI shipping within Sketch was that designers would no longer need to search the Internet to find it and then import it into the program. It would now be easily accessible with the click of just a few buttons. To access the GUI, go to File in the menu above the toolbar and select New From Template, as shown in Figure 2-3. Select the appropriate template for which you are designing. You should see the templates for iOS app icon and iOS UI Design Mac App icon among others. Select the iOS UI Design Template, and you should be ready to go.

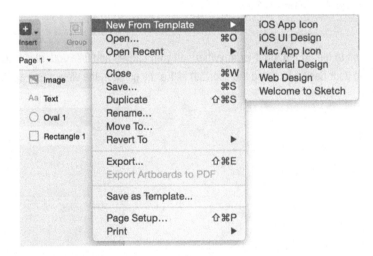

Figure 2-3. Accessing the Teehan+Lax iOS8 GUI from within Sketch 3

Once you've opened the menu and selected iOS UI Design from the drop-down, Sketch will open a new window with the template and all of the elements, layers, groups, and vectors, as shown in Figure 2-4. Layers and groups have been titled according to their corresponding elements on the canvas. Hovering your mouse over an element in the Layers list will highlight the corresponding element on the canvas. Here you have all of the UI elements that you'll need to design an app for iOS.

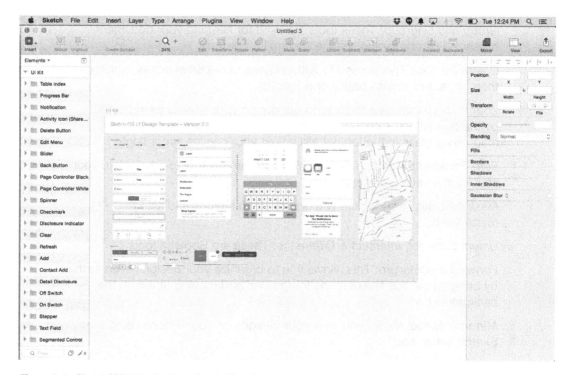

Figure 2-4. *Sketch iOS UI Design Template in Sketch 3*

If you're starting a new design or mockup for iOS, you can easily jump right in by adding any of these elements onto your artboard, right from your toolbar. Simply open the template and go to: **Insert ➤ Symbols** and select an individual symbol that you'd like to add to your design.

Because the canvas is completely unconstrained, when designing for particular devices, screen sizes, and resolutions, this could present issues. How do you design for a small screen versus a larger one, an iPhone as opposed to an iPad, or even for a monitor on which a website will be displayed? This brings us to our discussion and exploration of artboards.

Toolbar

The *toolbar*, shown in Figure 2-5, contains all of the tools that you need to make your designs. You'll be using the toolbar to create shapes and to add layers. As you examine the toolbar, the Insert menu on the far left is the first button you'll see. The Insert menu will be used for creating shapes, adding text, images, artboards, and so forth. All of these elements will become building blocks of any design that you create with Sketch.

Figure 2-5. The Sketch toolbar appears along the top of the canvas

From left to right, the additional elements in the toolbar are as follows. We will discuss each in more detail later in the book:

> *Group and Ungroup*: These tools are used for keeping your document organized by combining selected layers into groups.

> *Create Symbol*: This is used to flatten layers to create symbols, which can then be reused across pages or artboards.

> *Zoom*: This allows you to zoom in our out on your canvas as indicated by the percentage sign. Clicking the plus or minus button next to the magnifying glass in the toolbar will adjust your canvas accordingly.

> *Edit, Transform, Rotate & Flatten*: You can use this tool to manipulate your shapes in a variety of ways.

> *Mask & Scale*: This tool lets you clip layers to shapes and also to resize them.

> *Union, Subtract, Intersect & Difference*: These are Boolean tools.

> *Forward & Backward*: This allows you to organize your designs even further by bringing various layers to the foreground and moving others to the background.

> *Mirror*: This tool allows you view your designs on your iPhone using the Sketch Mirror app.

> *View*: This lets you show and hide various visual aids such as rulers, grids, and layout guides. You can also adjust grid and layout settings here.

> *Export*: This tool allows you to export your designs in a variety of different sizes.

Customizing the Toolbar

The toolbar can also be customized depending on your taste and workflow. Customizing the toolbar is helpful once you know which tools you use more often than others. It makes specific tools easy to access.

To customize the toolbar, go to the View menu and select Customize Toolbar. A window with all of the icons representing actions will slide down. You may add any of these icons to your toolbar simply by selecting the icon from the drop-down panel and dragging in into the empty spaces in your toolbar, as shown in Figure 2-6. Once you drag it into the space, it will snap into place. When you have selected all of the icons that you want, click Done and the drawer will roll up. For the remainder of this book, however, we will assume the existing default toolbar.

Figure 2-6. *Customize your toolbar by selecting icons from the drop-down panel*

Layers

There are a few different types of *layers* in Sketch. Layers are the building blocks of your apps. You will add various elements to your layers to create the different views in your applications. Typically, a layer will consist of a combination of shapes, text, and images. Sketch will tell you what kind of element is included in each layer by showing you a tiny symbol next to each. Shape layers will have a shape, text layers will show a small AA, and layers with images in them will contain a small image of a picture. These icons will allow you to identify easily what each layer consists of.

The Layers list shown in Figure 2-7 displays all of the layers in the canvas, and you can organize them there. Any layer can be selected and moved around the canvas. The list will populate as you add more layers. If you add a new shape onto your canvas, you will see that a new layer will be created on top. Sketch will automatically name the layer according to the shape that you have created. Layers can overlap each other, and you can manipulate which layer appears on top or behind each other directly from the Layers list. You can also do this by using the Forward and Backward buttons in the toolbar.

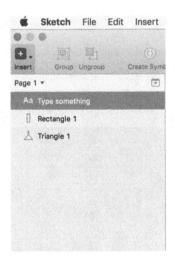

Figure 2-7. *The Layers list shows all of the elements on your canvas*

Selecting and Moving Layers

Layers are fairly flexible, and they can be moved around your canvas at any time. To select a layer, you can either choose the layer's name in the Layers list or select the specific layer on the canvas. Once you have selected a layer, you can move it around the canvas. You will know that a layer is selected by the appearance of white *handles*. These handles allow you to change the shape and the properties of the shape in that layer. Once you have selected a layer, you can use either the Inspector position properties, as shown in Figure 2-8, to move it around, or you can use your mouse to drag it around your canvas.

> **Tip**   To move a layer incrementally by a single pixel, use the arrow keys on your keyboard. To move a shape incrementally by 10 pixels, hold down Shift and press the arrow keys.

Figure 2-8. An image and two shapes on the Sketch canvas. Note that each object has a corresponding layer in the Layers list on the left

Duplicating a Layer

There are a number of ways that layers can be duplicated in Sketch. Right-click the layer in the canvas to reveal a new menu list, and select duplicate from that list. With this done, you will see that a new later has appeared in the Layers list. The new shape will appear on top of the duplicated shape in the canvas. All you need to do is to move it. Alternatively, you can create a new layer by holding down the Option key and clicking and dragging the layer to duplicate it.

Hiding and Locking Layers

When designing, it sometimes becomes necessary to hide layers so that you can effectively work on a given layer without being distracted or obstructed by others. Sketch allows you to do this easily. To hide a layer, hover your mouse over the right side of the cell in the Layers list. A small "eye" will appear. When it does, click it. You will see that the corresponding shape will disappear from the canvas. However, it will remain in the Layers list. Any layer that has been hidden will have greyed-out text and an icon of an eye next to it.

You might have a need to lock a layer for similar reasons. Sometimes, designers will lock their background layer to prevent it from interfering with the work they are doing on other layers. Since it is unlikely that the background will change, it can sometimes be locked but still remain visible to prevent accidental editing. To lock a layer, right-click and select Lock

Layer from the menu. You will see that a Lock icon will appear next to the corresponding layer in the Layers list. This icon denotes that the layer is locked from editing. Simply clicking the lock again will unlock the layer and allow it to be edited. Figure 2-9 shows a hidden image layer and a locked text layer.

Figure 2-9. The canvas with the image layer hidden and the text layer locked

Groups

Within your layers, you can also create *groups*. Groups are a great way to organize you designs. For instance, if you have multiple layers that make up the tab bar in your app, you might want to group all of the elements.

To create a group, select all of the layers that you want to group. You can select multiple layers by selecting and dragging a box around all of the elements that you would like to group. Alternatively, you can hold down the Shift key and select all of the layers in the Layers list that you would like to group. With all of the layers selected, click the Group button in the toolbar. You will notice that a folder has been created in the Layers list. Clicking the folder will reveal the various layers that make up the group.

Groups can also be nested. That is to say, there can be groups of layers within other groups. For example, if in your Tab Bar group you have five icons, you may want to create a group of icons within that group. The icon group folder will then be located within the Tab Bar group folder.

> **Tip**   You can move a group of shapes in a layer as one by opening the group and dragging it around the canvas.

Inspector

The *Inspector*, located on the far right of the user interface, as seen in Figure 2-10, shows you various properties of the selected layer on your canvas. Depending on what you have selected, it will show you information such as size, color, and styles. The Inspector contains the tools that allow you to view properties of selected objects on the screen. If you select an image, you will see properties pertaining to that image. If you select text, you will see properties pertaining to that body of text. If you change anything in your document, you will notice that the properties in the Inspector can and will change. To edit a shape, you can work directly within the Inspector to change values. These include position and size.

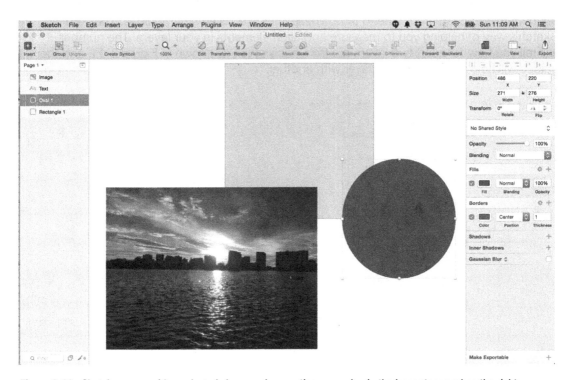

Figure 2-10. Sketch canvas with a selected shape and properties appearing in the Inspector panel on the right

Styles

You can adjust the *styles* associated with your layers in the Inspector. Take the circle in the Figure 2-9. Note that it is a solid red color. That color is associated with a Fill setting in the Inspector. The check box next to Fill setting has been selected. The color in that window is directly associated with the color of the circle. Clicking the red square next to fill will bring up a pop-over with a number of different fill options for the layer. Clicking anywhere in the area on the pop-over allows you to change the shade of the color of the layer. You can use the sliders below the color area to change the color, or to make it more or less opaque. The color picker allows you to sample any color on your screen inside or outside of Sketch. Below the color picker, you can edit the RGB or hexadecimal codes as well.

The icons along the top of the pop-over represent different options for the texture of the fill. The options range from left to right from solid fill, radial gradient, angular gradient, pattern fill, and noise fill.

Border color can also be edited and changed for thickness as well as other settings. There is also an option to add a shadow (outer or inner) to your shape by making selections in the Inspector panel.

Smart Guides

When moving shapes around on your canvas, you may notice some red lines with a number on them that appears from time to time. These lines are called *smart guides*. They are Sketch's way of helping you to measure and align elements in your layers. The number will tell you how far apart two layers are from each other, as shown in Figure 2-11, and the guides will help you to align one layer with another.

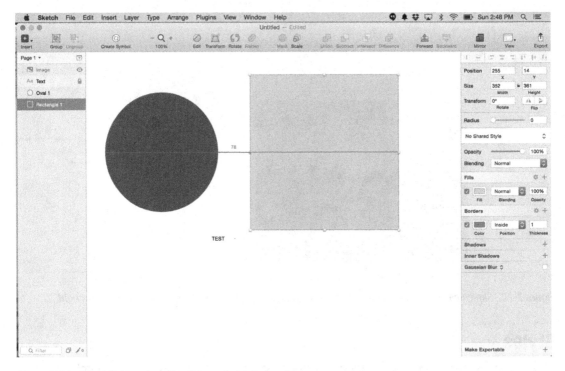

Figure 2-11. Smart Guides show the distance between two layers

Tip Holding the Option key down while you hover your mouse over two layers will show you the distance between two layers and whether or not they are aligned.

Artboards

If you've used Adobe Illustrator, you are probably familiar with concept of the artboard. An artboard allows you to define boundaries for your Sketch infinite canvas. It will create set dimensions that map to a specific device or screen for you to work within.

You can create an artboard in Sketch by going to the Insert button at the top left and selecting Artboard from the menu. You can create your own artboard or, luckily for those designing for iOS, Sketch comes with pre-sized templates, which make it easy to jump right in. This way, all you need to do is to select the appropriate size for your design and go.

You can create an entire application in one artboard in Sketch, which is very helpful. It's a handy way to see how your entire app will look without moving through a number of different files for each screen. It also adds some constraints to Sketch's infinite canvas. An artboard will create a boundary that is the correct size, depending on the device you are targeting.

After you've selected Artboard from the Insert button menu, the various templates will appear on the left side of your Sketch window. Sketch provides templates for the iPad (portrait, landscape, and Retina) and iPhone (portrait, landscape, and Retina), as shown in Figure 2-12. There are also templates for iOS icons.

Figure 2-12. Preset artboard templates in Sketch 3

You will note that selecting an artboard template will add the appropriate artboard on your canvas and also place a layer in the left layer panel. The titles of the layer will correspond to the template. To change the name of the layer, you can double-click it and rename it as you would any other file.

If you select a template for say, the iPhone, Sketch will create an artboard in the appropriate size to this device. You can also have multiple kinds of artboards in one canvas. This is helpful if you are creating, for instance, a universal app that will need to run on the iPhone and the iPad. In this case, you can add the template for an iPhone and an iPad and show how the app will appear on both devices. It's a nice way to present your work.

You can rearrange, duplicate, and even export your artboards in order to accommodate your designs. With Sketch, there are a few ways to duplicate artboards. You can copy and paste your artboard and line it up manually using the guides, or you can use Sketch's handy Make Grid feature. This feature allows you to duplicate your artboards with a few clicks. Simply select Arrange from the menu and choose Make Grid from the drop-down, as shown in Figure 2-13. Select the number of artboards that you want to duplicate by changing the numbers in the Rows and Columns fields, and select Make Grid when done. Sketch will automatically duplicate the artboard according to your selections and align them on your canvas.

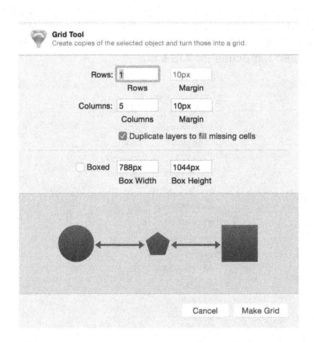

Figure 2-13. The Make Grid feature in Sketch 3 will help you to duplicate and align your artboards

Your artboards on your canvas make up the overall anatomy of your design. Sometimes, however, you will want or need to separate artboards. For example, if your design is incredibly complex and you want multiple artboards to represent a particular flow, it might be beneficial to break your design out into multiple pages, which Sketch supports. In the upper-left corner of your canvas and above the Layers list, you will see that you are currently working on Page 1. To add a page, simply click the button to the right that looks like a downward-facing arrow. Once you click that, the button will turn into a plus (+) sign, and this will allow you to add subsequent pages to your design.

Rulers and Guides

Upon first opening Sketch, you won't see any rulers or guides. This is because they are hidden by default. You can access the rulers by going to the View icon in your toolbar. This will reveal a drop-down menu that allows you to choose from a selection of rulers, grids, and other layout options, as shown in Figure 2-14. The option to show pixels is also in this menu. The purpose of these tools is to help you to align the elements in your design properly.

Here are the various selections and what they mean:

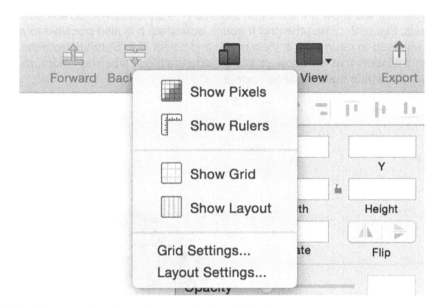

Figure 2-14. The View menu drop-down after expansion from the toolbar

Show Pixels

The *Show Pixels* option will show your element on the screen in pixel mode. This is helpful if you want to see how vector-based design will appear in pixels, such as in a browser.

Show Rulers and Guides

Because of Sketch's infinite canvas, the rulers are not fixed as in other graphic design programs. This means that you can move them around to accommodate your designs. For example, if you are designing for a screen not included in the preset artboard templates, you can create the dimensions on your canvas and use them as a guide in your design. Naturally, if you move the zero point in Sketch's ruler, anything before it will be shown in negative numbers. Figure 2-14 shows a Sketch canvas that has its rulers adjusted. If for some reason you need to reset the ruler, simply click the space where the horizontal and vertical ruler lines intersect. This should revert the rulers back to their original measurements.

You can add a guide to your canvas by clicking anywhere on the ruler. The guides will appear as red lines, and they will remain there until you remove the ruler. Figure 2-14 has guides and rulers activated. The zero point has also been adjusted on both the horizontal and vertical rulers.

Show Grid

When activated, the *Show Grid* function will create gridlines on your canvas. This is a typical grid with squares drawn by intersecting lines as is customary in most graphic programs. By default, the grid size will show a thick black line every 10 squares. The default size of the grid is 20 pixels. Figure 2-15 has the grid function activated. It is also possible to adjust this setting. You will need to return to the View menu and select Grid Settings from the menu. This will open a window that will allow you to change the block size and colors, as well as the frequency with which the thick lines appear.

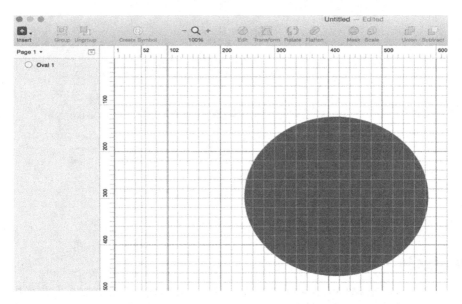

Figure 2-15. Gridlines on a canvas in Sketch

Show Layout

The *Layout* grid is another kind of grid available in Sketch. It allows you to define columns and rows. If you are using Sketch for Web design, your grid settings will be different and you might need to use the layout grid instead. These grids can also be modified to suit your needs.

Shortcuts

Before we dive deeper into Sketch, you will want to learn at least some of its *shortcuts*. They will greatly improve your workflow and reduce the amount of time it takes for you to perform certain actions. As a Mac user, you are likely already familiar with general shortcuts such as copy and paste. The following is a comprehensive list of Sketch shortcuts gathered from around the Web. In addition to the ones that are listed in the menu, you can use this as a reference until some of the more frequently used shortcuts become familiar to you.

General Sketch Shortcuts

^L	Toggle layout
^G	Toggle Grid
Enter	Edit currently selected layer
⌘2	Zoom to selected layers
⌘3	Center selected layer on canvas
⌘+	Zoom in
⌘-	Zoom out
⌘1	Center canvas
⌘2	Zoom selection
Z	To zoom, hold down and click or drag area with mouse
⌥Z	To reverse zoom, hold down and click
Esc	Exits current tool or mode
Space	Hand tool
Tab	Cycles through layers in the current group
Shift + Tab	Reverse cycle

Layer Shortcuts (Insert)

R	Rectangle
O	Oval
L	Line
U	Rounded rectangle
T	Text layer
V	Vector

P	Pencil
A	Artboard
S	Slice

Moving, Hiding, and Resizing Layer Shortcuts

⌥+ **Drag**	Duplicate layer
⌥+ **Hover**	Show distance between layers
⌥+ **Resize**	Resize from both ends
⇧+ **Resize**	Preserve aspect ratio
⌘ **Shift L**	Lock or unlock layer
⌘ **Shift H**	Hide or show layer
⋯→	Move
⌘⋯→	Resize

Text and Type Shortcuts

Cmd + B	Bold
Cmd +I	Italic
Cmd + U	Underline
Alt + CMD (+) +	Increase font size
Alt + CMD (+) -	Decrease font size

Custom Shortcuts

As a Mac user, you also may be familiar with custom shortcuts.

Control R	Toggle Rulers on and off
Control G	Toggle Grids on and off
Control P	Toggles between pixel and vectors
Control L	Toggles alignment guides

You can also create custom shortcuts for those actions that don't have them. Because Sketch is designed to work within the Mac OS, you can easily create your own shortcuts. For example, you may or may not notice that Insert Image has no shortcut in Sketch. You can easily create a shortcut consisting of your own keyboard combination. To create a custom shortcut, go to System Preferences and select Keyboard. From the tab at the top of the window, select App Shortcuts, as shown in Figure 2-16.

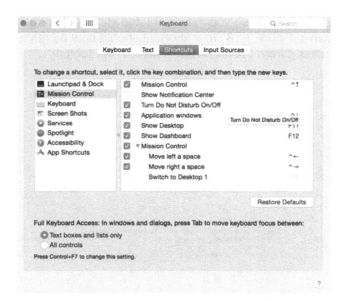

Figure 2-16. *You can create a custom shortcut from within your computer's System Preferences*

Once you have made these selections, click the "**+**" button near the bottom of the widow. A new drop-down should appear with a list of all of the applications on your computer. Scroll down and find Sketch in that list. In the field entitled Menu Title, type the exact title of the menu item for which you would like to create a shortcut, as shown in Figure 2-17. Finally, in the field called Keyboard Shortcut, enter the appropriate keys for your new shortcut and click the Add button. Your shortcut will not work if typed incorrectly.

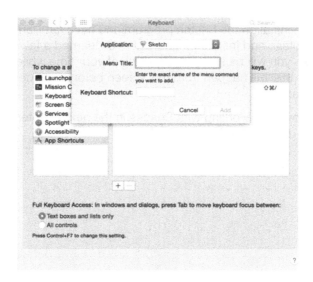

Figure 2-17. *Creating a menu title for your keyboard shortcut*

Once it has been added, you will see your newly created shortcut it in the list of shortcuts for that program, as shown in Figure 2-18. Your shortcut should now be ready for use in Sketch. You will be able to access it from the drop-down menu in the toolbar.

Figure 2-18. Creating a custom keyboard shortcut

We've now been through the entire Sketch interface. Thus you should be fairly comfortable with the essential functions of everything that you see on the screen when you open the program and with customizing your toolbar to your liking. As you can see, though the interface is simple, Sketch is a powerful graphics program that will make designing your iOS app a pleasurable experience.

Summary

Congratulations! You've installed the Sketch program and have familiarized yourself with the canvas, the toolbar, and Inspector, and you even learned a few handy keyboard shortcuts. This is where you will be spending the bulk of your time while designing in Sketch. Everything you do after this will happen from this screen before your design begins to come to life right on the canvas.

Now you're ready to move into working with Shapes in the next chapter. Shapes are the building blocks of your design. Read on!

Chapter 3

Styling Shapes

By this point you've had some time to interact and become more familiar with the Sketch interface. This chapter focuses on the shapes that you can create with Sketch. Shapes are the most important layers that you will use in Sketch, and every design you create in Sketch will be made of shapes that you choose from the Insert menu. They are the building blocks of any design that you will work on in Sketch.

As mentioned in the Chapter 2, you can use the Insert tool from the menu to add shapes to your canvas, or you can draw them directly onto your canvas using your mouse, trackpad, or graphics tablet. There are eight different kinds of shapes that can be created within Sketch: lines, arrows, rectangles, ovals, rounded rectangles, stars, polygons, and triangles. All of these options can be found in the **Insert ➤ Shape** menu, as shown in Figure 3-1. With these shapes, you can pretty much create anything.

Figure 3-1. Clicking Insert ➤ Shape on the toolbar provides a list of preset shapes that are available within Sketch

Once you select what shape you want, simply click and drag your mouse anywhere on your canvas that you want your shape to appear. Sketch will begin to create that shape with the default color (usually light gray for the fill and a darker gray for the border). When you release the mouse button, your fully formed shape will be complete and on the canvas. You will also notice that the Layers list will be updated to reflect the name of the layer (usually the name of the shape and the number 1 for starters). The numbers will increase in increments of one as you continue to add unnamed layers. As long as the shape is selected, the Inspector will also update to show you the properties associated with your shape. Pay particular attention to the values in Position, Size, Opacity, Fills, and Borders. If you change or edit any of these values in the Inspector, Sketch will automatically update the shape to reflect these changes.

Special Shapes

Some of these shapes have special settings in the Inspector. For example, the rounded rectangle shape will have additional Inspector settings for editing its corner radius. Setting the radius to 0 will yield no rounded corners and create a square, while the maximum setting of 40 will yield a rectangle with very rounded corners.

> **Tip**   To create a perfect square or circle, hold down the Shift key as you create your shape. This will constrain the proportions of the shape.

The star shape will have additional settings: a radius and a point setting become available in the Inspector, which will automatically update the number of points on the star as well as the center radius of that shape. The radius of the star refers to the distance from the center of the star. The points refer to the number of points on the star. The default point setting for the star, however, is 5. Changing the point setting to the maximum of 50 will increase the number of points on the star. The radius in Figure 3-2 is set to 50 percent, and the number of points is set to 10.

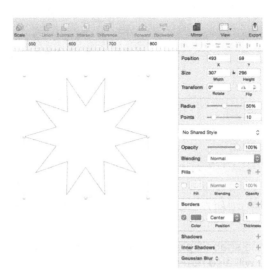

Figure 3-2. A 10-point star with a 50-percent radius

The polygon shape also has a point setting that will allow you to change the number of points from the default of 5 to a maximum of 10.

Editing Points on Shapes

To understand shapes fully, you must also understand points. *Points* are the basic elements of shapes. That is to say, points make up shapes. The line that connects two points is called a *path*. Thus paths combine two points to create shapes. A shape, then, is a collection of paths on a point.

Sketch also lets you edit the points of existing shapes on a canvas. After drawing your shape, select it and you will see the white handles that allow you to transform the shape. These handles, located at the top, bottom, and corners of the shapes, allow you to adjust the size of each shape manually. Adjusting these handles will increase or decrease the size of the shape in height and width accordingly. Adjusting the handles at the corners of a shape will alter both height and width.

But what if in the course of your work you find that you'd like to move the actual points in shapes to change them? Simply double-click the shape. You will notice the handles disappear and that they change to points. There will be multiple points depending on the shape. The Pen tool will also appear on your canvas when you hover your mouse over the intersection points of the shape, as shown in Figure 3-3.

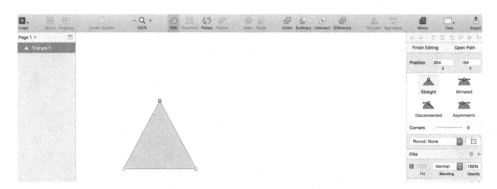

Figure 3-3. Double-clicking a shape will let you adjust the points. Note the Bezier curves in the Inspector

This will allow you to edit the shape's points based on the tool that you select in the Inspector on the right. You will also notice that once the shape's points become editable, four new selections will appear in the Inspector as well. These four different modes allow you to manipulate those points in various ways. These modes are: Straight, Mirrored, Disconnected, and Asymmetric. In Figure 3-4, the triangle from Figure 3-3 has been adjusted using the Mirrored Bezier curve.

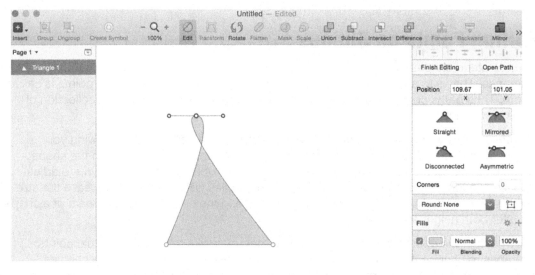

Figure 3-4. A triangle shape's points are edited using the Mirrored mode tool

Straight Mode

The *Straight* tool allows you to edit a path along a straight line with no handles or curves along the control point.

Mirrored Mode

This mode provides two opposite and mirrored points that appear the same distance from the main point and at the same angle. Sketch will remove any corners along the shape.

Disconnected Mode

This mode creates two points that are independent of each other. You can change each handle's point without affecting the other.

Asymmetric Mode

This mode is similar to Mirrored mode, but the distance between the main point and the control point will be independent.

Once you have made the points editable, you can click anywhere on that line between any two points to create a new editing point, and so forth.

> **Tip**   To escape this or any other mode, hit the Esc button.

Combined Shapes

There will be times when Sketch's ready-made shapes aren't exactly what you need in your designs, and it is necessary to combine shapes to get what you want. Sketch lets you to combine shapes to create unique forms that aren't included right out of the box, or that aren't immediately available, using the Insert menu. You can do this by dragging a shape on top or over another, selecting them both with your mouse, and clicking Union in the toolbar. Doing this will combine both shapes. Once they have been combined, as shown in Figure 3-5, they will behave as one solid unit.

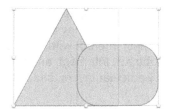 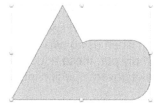

Figure 3-5. A triangle and a rounded rectangle before and after being combined by using the Union button

> **Tip**   Once two shapes have been combined, they appear as a group in the Layers list. A folder icon indicates a group. If you open the folder, you can access the two separate shapes once more and edit them as needed.

Custom Shapes

Sketch also makes this easy to create your very own *custom shapes*. Go to **Insert ➤ Vector** from the toolbar. The pointer will turn into a Pen tool. You can use this tool to create custom lines and custom points. You can click anywhere on your canvas to create multiple points for your custom shape.

You can also use the Transform tool to distort your shapes by changing its points. When using the Transform tool on a shape, you will notice that the opposite side will always move in tandem and in the opposite direction. The Transform tool is often used to create a perspective view of rectangular or square shapes. It has, however, a more flattening effect on circles and ovals.

> **Tip**   The default Transform mode will move both sides of your shape at the same time. To move only one side in one direction, hit the ⌘ key while dragging the desired corner of your shape.

Boolean Operations

There will be times while designing when you need to create a custom shape. Further, it might be a bit of a challenge to create some unique shapes using the vector tool. Sometimes, it is only possible to create this unique shape by combining two existing shapes in a unique way. This is the perfect opportunity to learn about another one of Sketch's handy features called *Boolean Operations*.

Boolean Operators are available in many graphics programs, including Photoshop. Thus if you're fairly adept at Photoshop, you should be familiar with the term Boolean Operators and what it means. For those of you who are not Photoshop users, a simple way of thinking about Boolean Operators when it comes to design software is that they allow you to create more complex shapes that consist of multiple paths. They allow you to group multiple paths together into more complex paths upon which Boolean Operators can be implemented.

Boolean terms are represented in the Sketch toolbar by buttons that have been conveniently grouped together in their own section, as illustrated in Figure 3-6. They represent actions that can be taken when using two or more shapes that must interact with each other in a specific way. Simply put, these actions include Add, Subtract, Intersect, and Difference. All four of these tasks govern specific interactions among particular layers, shapes, and paths.

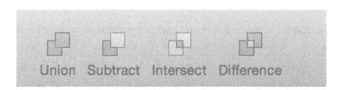

Figure 3-6. Boolean Operator buttons in the Sketch toolbar

A similar concept applies to Sketch. The icons associated with these buttons, as well as the manner in which they are grouped in the toolbar, are great indicators as to their use. To illustrate the effects of Boolean Operators, we will begin with two circle shapes, side by side, one slightly overlapping the other, as shown in Figure 3-7. We will then select both shapes by holding down the Shift key and selecting each shape, or by dragging a container around both shapes. You should see handles around each shape.

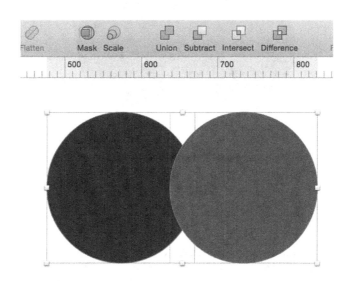

Figure 3-7. Two slightly overlapping circles illustrate the various Boolean Operators in Sketch. Note that both are selected

Union

The *Union* tool combines any two shapes. To use to the Union tool, select both shapes. Then click the Union button in the toolbar. As the image and its name implies, both shapes will be merged together to create one new shape. As shown in Figure 3-8, the new shape will have properties of both shapes. Nonetheless, you will still be able to edit both shapes individually if you so desire.

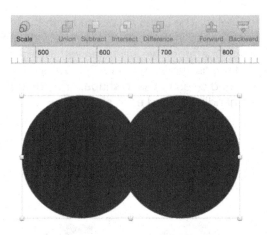

Figure 3-8. *The effect of the Union Boolean Operator on our two demonstration circles. Both shapes have been merged into one new shape*

Subtract

The *Subtract* tool will mask an area of overlapping shapes, thereby creating a new shape that is the result of the shape on top being removed from the one underneath it. Since our bright red circle was overlapping the darker red circle, it has been subtracted from the resulting shape. What remains now is the darker red circle minus the area where it overlapped with the other, as seen in Figure 3-9.

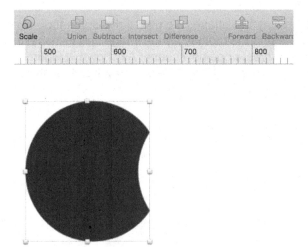

Figure 3-9. *The effect of the Subtract Boolean Operator on two overlapping circles*

Intersect

The *Intersect* tool highlights the negative space between two overlapping shapes to result in one new shape. Thus it appears that our two circles have disappeared, leaving only the space they both shared. What remains is created by the space where the two previously overlapped, as shown in Figure 3-10.

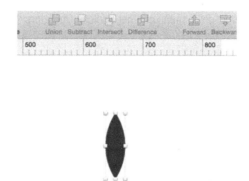

Figure 3-10. The resulting shape when using the Intersect Boolean Operator on two overlapping circles

Difference

The *Difference* tool highlights the negative space between two overlapping shapes as well, but displays the opposite effect of the Intersect tool. The resulting shape is shown in Figure 3-11.

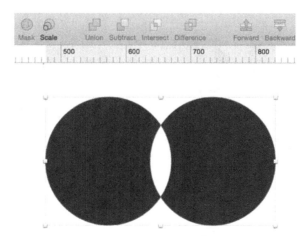

Figure 3-11. The resulting shape when the Difference tool is applied two adjoining circles

> **Tip**   Even though the icons in the Sketch toolbar represent the operations on squares and rectangles, a great way to think of how Boolean Operators work in Sketch is to visualize each operation as well as its effect on overlapping circles, the simplest of shapes.
>
> You can also switch Boolean Operators on a specific group of shapes from within the layers panel. Simply right-click a layer that has a Boolean Operators applied to it. You will see the current selection and a convenient drop-down menu of other Boolean Operators that you can apply.

Masks

Masking is a feature that can sometimes present issues for new designers. *Masks* in Sketch are a great way to add a unique element to an otherwise drab design. Masks are shapes that other objects can fit within. The great thing about masks is that you can use pretty much any shape to make a mask. You can use a mask, for instance, if you want an image to appear as though its outline has been carved into a certain shape, like a star or a circle. In so doing, that shape dictates the shape of the mask and, ultimately, how the masked image will appear. This kind of mask is known as an *Outline mask*.

When applying a mask to your canvas, every layer and shape in the selected group will be affected by that masking effect. Therefore, if you are attempting to mask specific layers but not others, it is best to move those layers out of a group.

For example, in Figure 3-12, you will see three items on the canvas. When a mask is applied by going to the Layer menu and selecting Use as Mask from the drop-down, all of the items except for the one that is selected "disappear" from view.

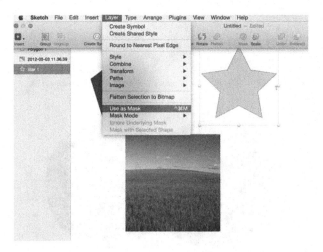

Figure 3-12. Selecting Use as Mask from the Layer menu lets you use one shape to mask others

Rest assured they haven't gone far. Sketch is applying the mask effect to everything on top of the image to be used as a mask. When this happens, they disappear. However, a quick check of the Layers list will show you that they are still on the canvas in their original positions. The Layers list will also indicate specifically which layers have had a mask applied to them with a small bullet to the left of the layer name.

Hovering your mouse over the layer will highlight the shape on the canvas. If you have a layer that is in the mask group but that you don't want to be affected by the mask, simply select it, go back to the Layer menu, and click Ignore Underlying Mask. You should then be able to see the shape without the effect of the mask, and the bullet will disappear from that layer.

Outline Mask

To see the masking effect in action, simply drag your new shape over the mask shape, as shown in Figure 3-13. You will see that a star mask has been applied to the image on the screen. The parts of the image that fall outside of the star will not be shown.

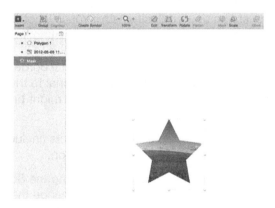

Figure 3-13. A masked image with the star shape

Alpha Mask

An *Alpha mask* allows you to apply a gradient effect as a mask. It works in the same way as the Outline mask. To see this effect, you need to select Alpha mask from your Layer drop-down, and you will need to edit the color gradient and settings in the Inspector at the right, since the gradient is what determines the fill, as opposed to the shape in the Outline mask. You can then adjust the transparency and select the appropriate gradient setting, depending on the effect that you would like to create.

Flattening

Flattening is the process by which you remove the hierarchy of paths and sub-paths that make up a shape. If you are familiar with other graphics programs, you may have gotten into the habit of flattening layers to reduce file size and possibly to improve performance, since large file sizes tend to slow down a computer. Sketch is no different in this respect. Multiple pages, artboards, and effects can slow things down significantly. However, if you have a number of shapes that consist of more than just a few sub-paths and intersects, it can be a good idea to flatten them in order to keep them as clean and consistent as possible, and it's just good design to do so. Flattening will remove extraneous vector points and Bezier curves and make your exported file smaller as well.

Scaling

Scaling in Sketch happens in two very distinct ways. Let's discuss them both since they will produce very different results on your shapes. If you have a particular shape on your canvas, arguably the easiest way to scale that shape up to make a bigger shape is to select and drag the handles of the shape to your desired size. You will notice that the dimensions in the Inspector will also adjust automatically as you are adjusting the corners of the shape. However, if you have a shape with an outline or effect attached to it, then dragging to scale will only increase the overall size of the total image. The actual border and any additional associated effects will not increase in a way that is proportional to the image. If that is your overall desired effect, then it is fine. However, if it is not, you might be wondering how to change this.

If you'd like to scale the shape as well as its associated effects (including borders, shadows, and other effects), then you will need to use the Scale function.

You can access the Scale function from the toolbar by clicking the Scale button. Once you've selected it, a window appears which allows you to change the dimensions of your shape. The window contains editable fields (height, width, and scale) which allow you to change their values, thus scaling the layer appropriately.

Figure 3-14 shows three green rectangles that I created on my canvas. From left to right, the first rectangle is the original. The second (center) was created by dragging the handles to create a rectangle that is roughly twice the size of the original. The third rectangle (right) was created using the Scale function and increasing the scale size from 100 to 200 percent. Note the difference between the second and third rectangles. The border around the third rectangle has increased proportionally to the size of the shape, whereas the border around the center rectangle is the same size as the original, even though the size of the rectangle has increased.

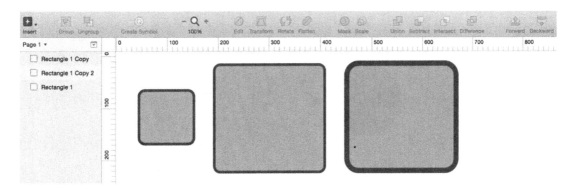

Figure 3-14. *Sketch's scaling feature in action*

Styles

Now that you've learned about the interface and styling, we'll dive a little deeper into details and functionality of the Inspector and attaching various styles to the shapes and layers in your designs. Your designs will likely consist of images and shapes. They will also, naturally, contain a variety of fills and borders, so we'll start with these.

Fills

While we briefly touched upon the fill feature in our earlier discussion of the Inspector, we will now explore this feature in greater detail. As mentioned earlier, most styling will take place in the Inspector, which is located on the right side of the Sketch canvas. Fill has a few additional properties associated with it. Specifically, when you have created a shape on your canvas, you can easily change the fill attribute by ensuring that the check mark next to the fill attribute is checked, and by clicking the default gray swatch next to it. This will reveal the color picker, which allows you to select pretty much any color in the spectrum as the fill color for the selected shape on your canvas. The shape then updates automatically with a solid color if none of the other selections have been activated.

There are other types of fills, of course, and they all appear as options for styling your layer once you select a fill and reveal the color picker pop-up. Beyond Solid Fill, there is Linear Gradient, Radial Gradient, Circular Gradient, Pattern Fill, and Noise Fill, as shown from left to right in Figure 3-15. An explanation of each type of gradient follows.

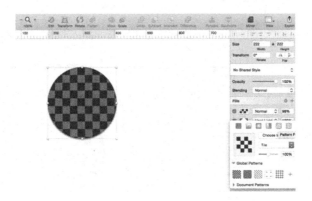

Figure 3-15. *A Pattern Fill style on an oval*

> **Tip**   To discover the name of each type of fill, roll over the appropriate box. After a moment, a pop-over with the name of the fill will appear.

Pattern Fill

This feature allows you to use an image or selection with a pattern as a fill. It's a nice way to give your design some texture. Sketch also comes with some preset textures that you can use in your design. An illustration of a *Pattern Fill* style is shown in Figure 3-15.

Noise Fill

An illustration of a *Noise Fill* style is shown in Figure 3-16.

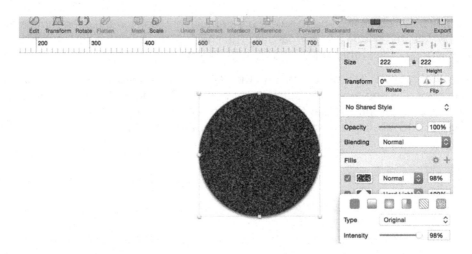

Figure 3-16. *Noise Pattern Fill on an oval*

Sketch allows you to add multiple levels of fills, and it also allows you to combine fills, colors, and gradients all on the same layer.

Now notice in Figure 3-17 that on the bottom of the pop-over in the Inspector Panel, there is a row of fields. From left to right, they should read Hex, R, G, B, A. Hex stands for hexadecimal code, which is a numerical representation of color in HTML and CSS. Every color has a different Hex code. The field above the word Hex is where Sketch allows you to enter the Hex code of a particular color instead of using the color picker. The letters stand for the colors Red, Green, and Blue. The letters below the color picker also let you know that Sketch is in RGB mode.

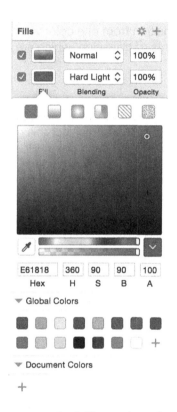

Figure 3-17. Inspector with fill attribute pop-over extended to reveal saved swatches, Hex codes, color picker, blending, opacity options, and gradients

Sometimes, you may see the letters H, S, and B below the color picker instead, as is shown in Figure 3-17. H, S, and B stand for Hue, Saturation, and Brightness, respectively.

If you move your cursor around within the color picker, you will notice that the values in the fields below (R, G, B or H, S, B) will change, as will the Hex code. If you are in HSB mode, moving the pointer towards the top increases the brightness, and moving the pointer left to right increases the saturation. Typically, you will want to be in HSB mode for designs.

Tip   You can toggle between RGB and HSB modes by holding down the Shift key and clicking the letters.

You can also save color swatches that you use often or plan to use in the future. Sketch automatically allows you to save color swatches right below the color picker by clicking the plus (+) sign at the lower-right corner of the color picker window. Sketch will also let you save a color swatch via the Eyedropper tool. This lets you select a color from anywhere on your screen, even outside the program.

Gradients

Gradients are a kind of fill that transition from one color to another. When using the Gradient tool, Sketch will show you the points of transition, which are editable right on your canvas.

Linear Gradient

As its name suggests, the *Linear Gradient* tool allows you to create a gradual blend from one color to another along a straight line. If you select this gradient, you will see two editable points in your layer in the canvas. Dragging each point will adjust the points on the gradient. You can also use the gradient bar in the Inspector to adjust points in your gradient. You may add points along the line as well simply by clicking anywhere along the line. Each point will represent a color stop of the gradient in your layer. These points allow you to edit and adjust the smoothness of the gradient on your layer. To delete a stop on the line, hit the Delete button. The Linear Gradient style is shown in Figure 3-18.

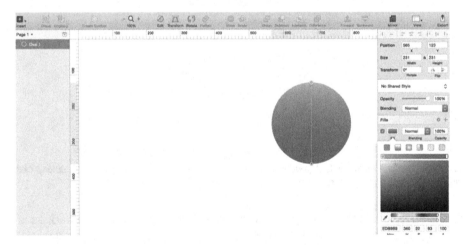

Figure 3-18. Linear gradient style

Radial Gradient

The *Radial Gradient* tool adds a larger circle to your layer. Within this larger circle, there will be two points: one in the center that sets the center of the radius, and the other outside of the radius, which controls its size. The Radial Gradient tool transitions from one color to another using a circular pattern or motion. You can expand the radius and shape of your gradient within the canvas as well. The Radial Gradient tool is shown in Figure 3-19.

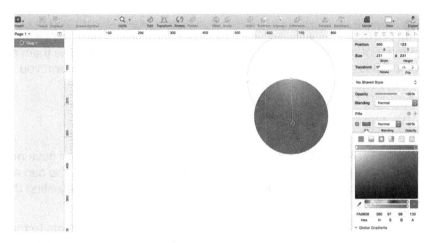

Figure 3-19. Radial Gradient tool

Circular Gradient

The *Circular Gradient* tool transitions clockwise around the center point of your layer. The Circular Gradient tool is shown in Figure 3-20.

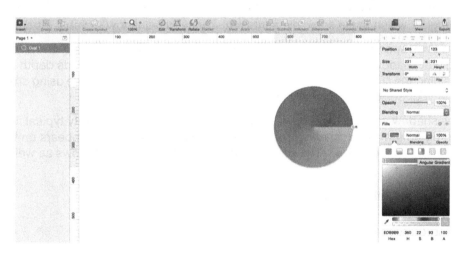

Figure 3-20. The Circular Gradient tool

Angular Gradient

The *Angular Gradient* tool transitions from one color to another in a counterclockwise direction around a specific point.

Blending

There are a number of different *blending* options available in Sketch. To see them all, you will need to click the fields above the blending option. A drop-down menu shows you a list of all of the blending options available for the selected shape.

Opacity

The *opacity* setting in Sketch is layer specific, meaning that each layer can have not only its own fill style and setting, but it can also have a different layer of opacity. You can adjust the level of opacity for the corresponding layer by clicking the number and adjusting the number (in percent) above the Opacity label.

One of the great things about Sketch is the ability to add a number of effects to the same layer. Thus you can add as many fills to one layer as you choose. They will stack up on top of each other from bottom to top. To add a fill, simply hit the + button to the right of the fill section in the Inspector.

Shadows

Shadows are great in designs because they can make your designs more three dimensional. Even if you are working on a flat design, a shadow can help make certain items in your design more pronounced. And even in a flat design, you must consider elements such as light and angles, which make some elements actually need a shadow—even if it's subtle.

While flat design specifically did away with the dreaded "drop shadow," lately the trend of using long, flat shadows in a flat design has become popular. This effect adds depth while still maintaining the "Flat" effect. For the most part, though, you will likely be using shadows minimally in your designs, specifically when designing for iOS.

Sketch has shadow settings that you will find in the Inspector that are pretty typical for graphics programs. You can change the settings for where your shadow appears on the x or y axis, the blur, and the spread. The same settings apply to the inner shadows as well.

> **Tip**   The spread feature is not available for text layers.

Blurs

Sketch has four different modes for the Blurring effect: Gaussian Blur, Motion Blur, Zoom Blur, and Background Blur. We will now discuss them in and will show you examples of a few of these blurs.

Gaussian Blur

The *Gaussian Blur* is a staple of most graphics programs, and it is used to reduce noise in an image as well as detail. The effect is an even, smooth blur across the affected layer— typically an image. The Gaussian Blur effect and all other blurs can be found at the lower-right corner of the Inspector. It is the first selection on the list of additional blur effects available in Sketch. You can adjust the amount of the blur in pixels using the provided slider, which appears when you select this effect. Figure 3-21 shows the original image on the left and the same image with the Gaussian Blur effect applied at 4 px.

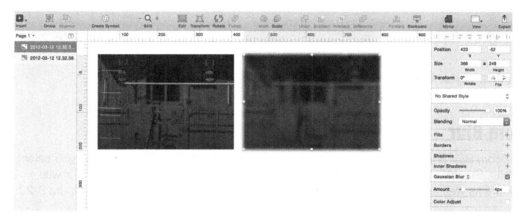

Figure 3-21. Original image on the left and the same image with the Gaussian Blur effect applied at 4 px

Motion Blur

As its name implies, the *Motion Blur* produces the effect of something that is in motion. This effect will allow you to blur in a particular direction. As with the Gaussian Blur, you can adjust the amount of the motion in pixels using the provided slider once you select this effect from the drop-down. You can also adjust the angle of the blur using the dial that appears once this option has been selected. The Motion Blur effect is illustrated in Figure 3-22.

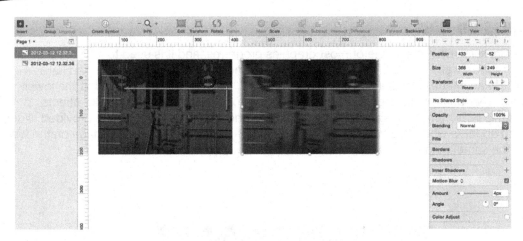

Figure 3-22. *Original image on the left with a Motion Blur effect applied on the right*

Zoom Blur

The *Zoom Blur* effect lets you blur a layer from a specified point outward. Once you select this blur, Sketch will present you with options to edit the point from which the blur will originate as well as the amount of pixels. The Zoom Blur effect is illustrated in Figure 3-23.

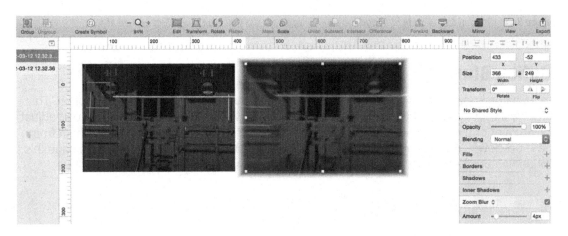

Figure 3-23. *A standard image on the left with no effect applied, and the same image on the right with the Zoom Blur effect applied*

Background Blur

The *Background Blur* effect was added by the Bohemian Coding team specifically after the iOS7 redesign. It is an effect that is used liberally throughout iOS, so you should feel comfortable about using it in your app designs. It blurs the background behind a shape but not the shape itself. The effect works best once you have reduced the opacity on the intended layer. Without this, the effect will be difficult to see.

The Background Blur effect will take a considerable toll on your computer's resources. You will see it slow down the program and your computer overall. Thus it's wise to use it sparingly.

> **Tip**   The Background blur function can be used to create a "frosted glass" effect, much like the Control Center that slides up from the bottom of your home screen on the iPhone.

Sharing Styles

At some point in your design experience, you will want to apply the same styles (shadows, fills, and so on) to a particular shape or object. With Sketch, this is possible to do in a few easy steps. But first, why would you want to do this? As a UI designer, you understand that speed and efficiency are paramount when designing interfaces. You will undoubtedly find yourself in a situation where both will come into play, and you will be required to be not only a skillful designer, but a fast and efficient one as well.

Sharing styles will help you with this. Consider for instance when you have a shape to which you have attached certain styles and you need to attach the same style or style to a different shape. First you can copy a style from one object to another by using the option+⌘+c key combination. This copies a style from one object. Then navigate to the new object, select it, and press the option+⌘+v key combination to attach the style to the new object. Note that this simply copies the style from one object to another. The objects, however, remain independent of each other.

If for some reason you need to share a style among multiple objects, you would then use the Sketch Shared Style function. This allows you to create a new style and attribute it to any new object or objects. The great thing about this feature is that once you create a style and attach it to an object, any additional changes to the style will update all objects to which it has been attached.

To create a new style, simply click the drop-down in the Inspector that reads No Shared Style, as shown in Figure 3-24. You can create a new shared style here, and it will automatically be associated with the selected object.

Figure 3-24. Creating a shared style by clicking the Shared Styles drop-down in the Inspector

Figure 3-25 shows two images side by side. One oval has a style attached to it and the other does not. To attach the style to the new oval, you must select the oval and the desired style from the style drop-down in the Inspector. The oval will automatically be updated with the new style and any additional changes moving forward, also as shown in the figure. The styles can be updated, deleted, or changed at any time. As long as a style has been attributed to an object, they will be updated with that new style.

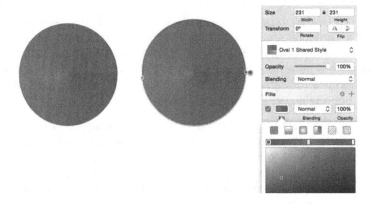

Figure 3-25. Two objects with a single style being updated

Images

As mentioned in the very first chapter of this book, Sketch is primarily for designers who want to create user interfaces for the Web and for mobile devices. Because it allows designers to work with vectors, Sketch is likely not the best option for image editing. As mentioned earlier, that was the initial purpose of Photoshop. Thus, in this instance, I recommend using it or any one of the other worthy alternatives when you need to do serious image editing.

That being said, there are some fairly decent basic image editing tools in Sketch if you need to do something related to images on the fly.

> **Tip**   Any selection of more than one layer can be combined into a bitmap by selecting Flatten Selection to Bitmap from the Layer menu.

Sketch has improved its image editing abilities (specifically for bitmaps) with version 3.X, and it has increased the number of image editing tools. The image editing tools are activated when you select an image or bitmap on the canvas and double-click it. You will notice that the Inspector updates to include tools that are specific to image editing. A selected image with the image editing tools on display is shown in Figure 3-26.

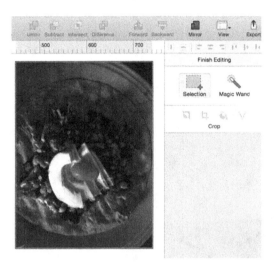

Figure 3-26. The new and improved bitmap editing tools in Sketch

The tools available for editing bitmaps are as follows:

> *Selection*: This tool allows you to select a rectangular area anywhere on your image.

> *Magic Wand*: This tool lets you select an area within an image by clicking and dragging.

> *Invert*: This tool lets you invert any previous selection.

> *Crop*: This tool lets you select an area of your image and exclude anything outside of the selected area.

> *Color*: This tool lets you select an area and fill it with any color selected from the available color picker.

> *Vectorize*: This tool will turn a selected area into a shaper layer of its own.

Color Adjust

While Sketch's ability to edit photos is limited, you can still do some minor adjustments. If you need to adjust colors of an image or bitmap, Sketch allows you to adjust the Hue, Saturation, Contrast, and Brightness of an image by moving sliders in the *Color Adjust* panel, which is shown in Figure 3-27. Once your image has been imported, click the box next to the Color Adjust heading in the lower-right corner of the Inspector, which will bring up the Color Adjust sliders.

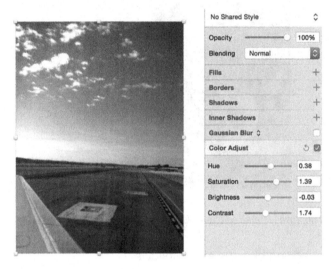

Figure 3-27. An image altered using the Color Adjust tool

Styling shapes is an important part of designing with Sketch, giving your designs character and your own unique touch. Take some time to become familiar with each style—and there are many—to understand how they can enhance your work. Experiment, mix, and match where you can.

Summary

Shapes are the building blocks of almost any design, and now that you understand how you can customize your shapes by using the available effects and styles, you are well on your way. Take some time to experiment with the styles and features that you've just learned about before you move on to the next chapter.

In the next chapter, we will cover symbols and text, which will add a new exciting dimension to your designs.

Symbols and Text

In the previous chapter, you learned about sharing styles between objects, and you used the option+⌘+c and option+⌘+v keyboard combinations to copy and paste styles between them. This is a helpful and simple way to share styles between multiple objects. In this chapter, we will discuss Symbols, a Sketch 3 feature that takes sharing styles to a whole new level and that will greatly improve your workflow.

Symbols are new to Sketch 3, and it was one of the features that designers were most excited about in the new release. The Symbols feature allows you to select and reuse groups of objects across pages and even artboards in your design. For designers, the Symbols feature was a game changer.

SmartObjects is the Photoshop feature most like Symbols in Sketch. They make designing easier, and they allow you to make nondestructive changes to an image or object. By converting your layer to a smart object in Photoshop, you gain much more flexibility within your design.

Those of you who are familiar with Fireworks will recall that everything was contextual, and you were able to edit layers by just clicking them. The properties panel would update (like in Sketch), and you could get on with the business of editing that layer. Fireworks also had the ability to apply styles to a master page that would then govern certain styles within the document, even if they were spread out over a number of different pages. These are the closest features that compare to Symbols in Sketch.

When designing user interfaces (UI), whether for mobile use or Web applications, there are bound to be many repeatable elements across screens. Menu bars, icons, and buttons are some of the most common of these. As designers, we go through multiple iterations of the many elements in a design. Being forced to change every single element would be incredibly time-consuming and inefficient. The Symbols feature greatly minimizes redundancies across pages and artboards in your designs. I would say that the Symbols feature in Sketch is closer to the Styles feature in Fireworks than it is to the SmartObjects feature in Photoshop.

To understand how the Symbols feature works, it helps to take a meta look at your design. Zoom out so that you are able to see multiple artboards in a single view. Look for the repeatable items across your design. What elements appear over and over across multiple screens, artboards, or even pages? You will find that some objects appear on every screen. Buttons, headers, and tab bars are common.

While you are able to duplicate a screen with its exact elements intact, simply duplicating an artboard or copying a style does not update all of the elements. How tedious would it be to have to update all of your icons if a client requested a slight change in color or size?

We discussed Groups in Chapter 2 when we talked about layers. You may recall that Groups consist of a number of layers that can be combined based on their context. You can group layers by selecting those that you want to group and then selecting the Group icon from the toolbar to complete the action. You will see that it has been completed when the layers are combined in the Layers list with a folder icon. Clicking this icon will reveal all of the layers in that Group.

Understanding Groups is important to understanding Symbols because Symbols are another kind of group of layers. Like Groups, Symbols are represented by a folder in the Layers list. However, the folder is purple, not blue, as shown in Figure 4-1. The image shows a group of layers, indicated by the blue folder, and a Symbol, indicated by the purple folder. You can also see the Group, Ungroup, and Symbol buttons in the toolbar.

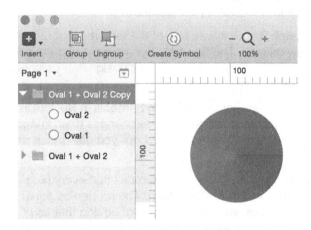

Figure 4-1. The Layers list showing a grouped set of layers, as well as a set of layers that have been made into a symbol

To create a symbol, you simply select all of the layers that will make up the symbol and click the Create Symbol button in the toolbar.

Tip   Another way to create a symbol is to go to the Layer menu and select Create Symbol.

If you are selecting multiple individual layers, Sketch will combine them into one group and create the purple folder in the Layers list on the right. Now that the symbol has been created, you are free to use and reuse that symbol across the various pages and artboards in your designs. Note that symbols cannot be used across different designs in different documents. If you'd like to use that or any other symbols across your design, you will need to go to the Insert menu and select Symbols from the drop-down, as shown in Figure 4-2.

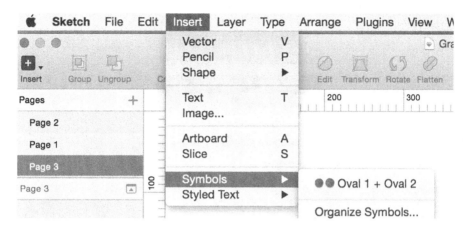

Figure 4-2. The Insert Symbols menu

It is also possible to create a Symbol from an already existing Group. Simply select the Group from the Layers list, and choose Create New Symbol from the Inspector on the right of the screen, as shown in Figure 4-3. The drop-down there will let you know that the currently selected layers are not a symbol and also show a list of the available symbols. Once you have created multiple symbols, you can also organize them from this menu.

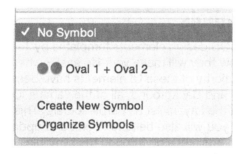

Figure 4-3. A list of available symbols and other symbol options

If you are working on a robust design, you may find that you have created a number of symbols over the course of working on the design, and the number can become very large. Sketch lets you organize your symbols easily with a Manage Symbols option. You access this option via the **Insert ➤ Symbol ➤ Manage Symbols** menu. The Manage Symbols option allows you to see a list of all of the symbols in your documents. You can then rename symbols or even delete them from this menu to keep track of them. There is also an option to organize all of your symbols from this menu. Simply select Organize Symbols from the **Insert ➤ Symbol** menu, and a window will provide you with options for organizing your symbols just the way that you want. The Organize Symbols window shown in Figure 4-4 is a handy tool that lets you sort all of your symbols.

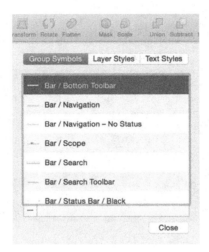

Figure 4-4. The Organize Symbols window

Tip   Symbols from the Organize Symbols menu are listed in alphabetical order.

iOS Template Symbols

In Chapter 2, we discussed iOS design elements templates by Teehan+Lax, which are now included in Sketch 3, and how they will make your life easier when designing for iOS. It is important to note that the majority of these UI elements have been added as symbols. With the exception of the Tab Bar and Background, all of the various iOS UI elements are all symbols, and they appear in the Layers list as purple folders. This means that as you build a page with these elements, you will also be able to edit and update these symbols across your design pages and artboards. Let's go through the symbols and set up an artboard for a basic app using some symbols from the iOS template.

Start with a new artboard from the iOS template by selecting the size of the device for which you are designing. I'll choose the iPhone 6 Plus. After selecting the size of the device, Sketch will add a new artboard in the appropriate size onto the canvas. You can now populate it with items such as a map, tab bar, status bar, and so forth. These symbols can make up a basic app page, as shown in Figure 4-5.

Figure 4-5. A simple UI created using symbols from the iOS template included in Sketch 3

Text and Fonts

We mentioned how symbols are linked globally across pages, artboards, and layers, so it makes sense to discuss text here since text styles work much in the same way as symbols do across pages and artboards. You already know that it is possible to manage multiple symbols and make changes to them on the fly as you iterate through your designs. Sketch also allows you to do this with text. Moreover, since Sketch 3 now uses the native font rendering for OS X, it means that text (especially text intended for the Web) looks great. But there's a whole lot more that you can do with text in Sketch 3, and this makes the difference between a good design and a great design.

Generally, typography in app design is important especially because of the limited real estate on which users must interact with content. While a font may look cool in your designs, you must always keep the user in mind. Accordingly, text in apps must remain legible at all times. It's also a good idea to make sure that your font sizes don't change from page to page. In this respect, you may want to create a style guide for your app before you proceed with the heavy lifting of the design. While creating a style guide can be tedious for designers who prefer to "just get on with it," it's a great practice and it helps to maintain a level of consistency—particularly when it comes to font and sizes—when handing off to other designers and developers alike.

For those designing for the Web, Sketch comes with a preloaded template that you can select when creating a new document. Much like the templates for icons for iOS (iPhone & iPad), Sketch includes a template for those who design UIs for the Web. There's even one for Material Design for those individuals who are designing for Android devices.

When you select a UI element from the preloaded iOS App template, associated styles are included, like text styles. Take for instance if you wanted to select the Push notification symbol and add it to one of your artboards. Once you copy the symbol over to your designs, you will likely need to edit the copy of the notification message. To do this, you select the symbol and double-click the text fields to edit the content.

As you can see in Figure 4-6, selecting a text field reveals the style associated with it in the Inspector. You can edit the copy in the symbol and keep the associated style. In the figure, the Style is listed as "Notification Content." However, that style can be changed to any other text style in the list, or even to one you create on your own. In this instance, you simply need to select the copy and select a new style from the drop-down menu.

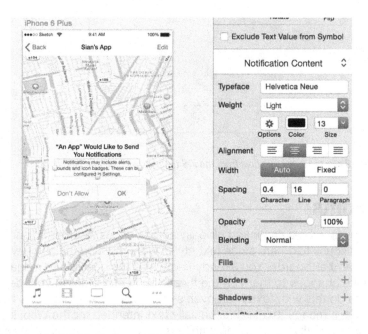

Figure 4-6. Selecting a text field highlights its associated style in the Text Inspector

> **Tip**   Since many of the styles in the template adhere to Apple's Human Interface Guidelines, you might want to leave them as is with minimal editing.

To insert text into an existing design, go to the Insert menu and select Text. This then turns your cursor into a text tool. Once the text tool appears, you can begin typing. Sketch will prompt you by inserting preformatted text on the canvas that reads "Type something," as shown in Figure 4-7. Once the text box appears, you are free to begin typing. The box will automatically expand to accommodate the additional text you type. What you can't see in the figure, however, are the handles around the text. Like any other layer in Sketch, text on a canvas gets its very own box with handles. Other layers have handles on all four sides, but the text box will have three. While in Auto mode, you can adjust these handles easily to change the size of the text just as you would with a shape, image, or vector. Pulling on the handles on the left or right side of the box will expand the text box and make it wider. When dragged, the handle on the bottom will make the text bigger or smaller within the box. This is a handy way of changing font size in your text field without adjusting the numbers in the Inspector.

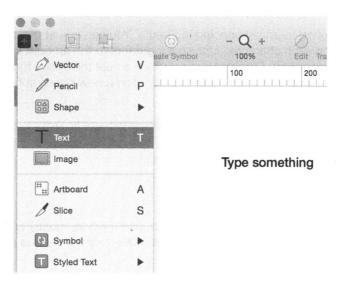

Figure 4-7. The default text tool on a blank canvas

Nonetheless, the text field can also be restricted by selecting the Fixed option in the Inspector to the right. There are a number of selections that you can make that will affect the text that you are typing on your canvas at that time. Currently, the text in the Figure 4-8 is set to resize the box automatically as you type, as the Auto button is highlighted. If the Fixed button is selected, then the size of the text box will be restricted and the text will wrap to fit within it.

Figure 4-8. A closer look at the Text Inspector options for styling your text layers

The Text Inspector

As with any other text editor, Sketch provides you with many ways to edit your fonts their weight, color, and size. When clicked, the Typeface option offers a list of all of the fonts on your computer as well as a preview of what each font looks like. To select one, simply click it. The weight will show the thickness or thinness of the font that you have selected, and there are other options, such as italics, light, bold, and black.

If you'd like to create text in underline or various list types, these can be found by clicking the Options button next to the color picker swatch. Sketch offers double-underlined text, bulleted, and numbered lists as options.

You also have the option to adjust spacing in Sketch. You can adjust the *character spacing*, or the space between each character. *Line spacing* refers to the amount of vertical space between multiple lines of text. *Paragraph spacing* will adjust the space that the program automatically assigns after you hit the return key to start a new paragraph.

> **Tip**   If you'd like to insert a line break instead of a paragraph break, hit Shift+Return instead of just Return when typing text.

Text Alignment

Alignment of text in Sketch is fairly straightforward, and it works mostly in the same way as in word processors and other graphics programs. You use the various settings to left or right-align your text, or to center or justify it.

Text on a Path

There are times when you will want to have your text aligned to something other than a straight line. You might want the text to follow a curve or a path. Sketch 3 accommodates this with the *Text on a Path* feature. First you create a vector or path that isn't straight. You can do this using the Vector tool or even using a shape like an oval. After you've created your shape, insert a text box and add some copy. With the copy selected, navigate to the Type menu and select the Text on a Path option. Once you move the text box closer to the desired shape or path, the copy will snap to the path along the curve, as shown in Figure 4-9.

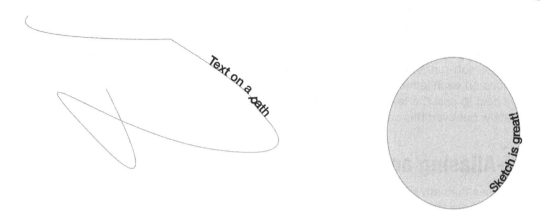

Figure 4-9. Text on a Path feature using a vector and an oval drawing

Text Outlines

Text Outlines is another great feature in Sketch that comes in handy when you're looking to do something unique. Text cannot be manipulated the way that you manipulate shapes or to attach certain operations. With the Text Outlines feature in Sketch, you can get text to behave like shapes. To use this feature, you can add a letter or letters to your canvas as an example. With the letters selected, navigate to the Type menu and select the Convert Text to Outlines option. If you only typed one letter onto your canvas, when you convert that selection alone to a Text Outline, you will see that handles are attached to the letter on the screen and the Layers list will update to represent the change. What has occurred is that Sketch has converted the text into a shape, as shown in Figure 4-10. You are now able to edit that letter, just as you would any other shape.

Figure 4-10. The before and after states of a text layer that has been converted to a shape using the Convert to Text Outlines feature

If you choose to convert more than one letter or a number of letters using the Text Outlines feature, bear in mind that this can use up your computer's resources. The reason for this is that converting long text items with multiple letters into vectors will require Sketch to create many small sub-paths. Creating sub-paths requires Sketch to calculate many Boolean operations on each letter in a string of text. If you must convert long text items, then it is always best to split the text into multiple layers. That way, you can convert each text item on separately, but even this can be taxing on your computer's resources.

Anti-Aliasing and Text

Sketch uses the native font rendering abilities of the Mac OS and, as such, there are some instances where the OS has no control over the appearance of text. In these instances, it will use sub-pixel anti-aliasing to improve the appearance of text on a screen. This means that red, green, and blue light are added to each pixel. Because each pixel is actually made up of red, blue, and green sub-pixels, the idea is that when observed from a normal viewing distance, such as the distance between you and the computer display, your eyes won't notice the colored pixels and will see the text as sharply as possible.

Sometimes, however, sub-pixel anti-aliasing and layer blending won't work because it needs to be drawn on an opaque background and rendered on a transparent background. When Sketch can't render fonts that are sub-pixel anti-aliased, like on an exported PNG, you will see it clearly because the background was transparent and could not be rendered.

Since, unlike the Mac OS, the iPhone does not render text with sub-pixel anti-aliasing, this presents some issues when designing for iOS. Since when designing your designs won't appear on the iPhone or iPad in the same way that they do your computer's screen (especially if you're designing on a Retina Mac), you will need to deactivate the anti-aliasing feature in your designs. (It is automatically selected by default.) You can disable it by navigating to the Sketch menu, selecting Preferences, and deselecting the option, as shown in Figure 4-11.

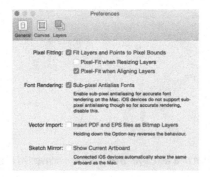

Figure 4-11. The Preferences pane in Sketch allows you to turn off the sub-pixel anti-aliasing feature for fonts

Text Styles

Sketch also allows you to attach styles to text, which you can easily apply to blocks of text in your designs. For example, while you may have the same font in use throughout your app, you may want different weights and sizes in different places, such as headers, body text, and so on. This is when text styles in Sketch can come in handy. You can apply an unlimited number of styles to layers in your document and easily manage them with the Text Inspector.

> **Tip**   Text styles are available *within* documents only. Thus they can be shared across pages and artboards, but NOT across different documents.

When you initially create text on the canvas, the Inspector will indicate whether or not a style has been attributed to the selected layer on the canvas. Usually, when adding text initially, there is no style. Once you add properties like color, size, case, and so forth, you can make these attributes into a style by selecting the drop-down in the Inspector, as shown in Figure 4-12.

Figure 4-12. The Text Inspector lets you create a new text style to assign to any text layer in your document

With the drop-down selected, Sketch allows you to create a new style. By default, the new style will be called whatever the text reads. Thus our new style here will be called "WE LOVE SKETCH Text Style," and it will be highlighted so that you can edit the style. You are then able to change the name of the style to whatever you choose. In Figure 4-13, I've changed the name of the text style to "Header Text Style."

Figure 4-13. The Text Inspector lets you to change the name of your style

Now if you are working on a completely new layer that contains text, you will be able to go to the Inspector, select the style you want to assign to it, and apply it.

You can also attribute a style to text by navigating to the Insert menu and selecting Styled Text from the drop-down menu, as shown in Figure 4-14.

Figure 4-14. Sketch lets you select saved styles from the Insert menu as well as the Text Inspector

Summary

Symbols are a great way to improve your workflow as you design your app. When designing for iOS, you can use the template included with Sketch to add native iOS symbols to your design. Sketch also offers the ability to manage these symbols as you use them across your design. Sketch also allows you to create and manage various text styles and effects for your designs.

Now that we've covered text styles and symbols, in the next chapter we'll talk about how to begin to prep for the design of your app by digging a little deeper into the Human Interface Guidelines created by Apple to help designers and developers understand best practices associated with iOS design.

Chapter 5

Prepping for App Design

So far, we have covered most of the basics of Sketch. You should now be familiar with the program and how it works—its interface, how to create basic shapes, and how to perform various design actions that will come in handy when you start designing your app. What we've done thus far is basically to expand upon the basic instructions and documentation provided by Bohemian Coding. This, however, does not an app make. In this chapter, we will prepare you for the actual design of your app.

The Human Interface Guidelines

The first thing that you want to do is to make sure that you have familiarized yourself with Apple's *Human Interface Guidelines (HIGs)*. Although I've alluded to them in previous chapters, if you haven't studied them, it's a good idea to do so now. I cover the HIGs in great detail in my previous book "Learn Design for iOS Development (Apress 2013). It's a great way to become familiar with the design standards that Apple has set forth for designers and developers who intend to create apps for iOS. Within these guidelines, Apple lays out its expectations and principles, which enable it to create a consistent experience across its mobile device ecosystem. Whether you are designing for the iPhone, iPad Air, iPad Pro, or iPad Mini, it is important to refer to and consider the HIGs as the ultimate guide and final word on design elements and principles for all of Apple's mobile devices.

> **Tip** You can access the Human Interface Guidelines for iOS on `http://www.developer.apple.com`.

When you design an experience for iOS consistent with the HIG principles, you increase the chances that your app will be successful because it uses elements and behaviors with which users are already familiar. While the HIGs have been covered to a degree previously, there are some principles that bear repeating before we get on with the business of designing your app.

Since its release with the first iPhone SDK, the documentation has evolved to accommodate the various versions of the software, most notably, iOS7 with its sweeping visual changes. It is a good idea to check them with each new release of the operating system. However, the main tenets of the guidelines—Deference, Clarity, and Depth—still remain. They are what give Apple its famous design aesthetic.

Deference

Roughly put, *deference* refers to creating a user interface that does not get in the way of other content on the screen. It is the very first theme introduced by Apple in the iOS HIGs, and it is arguably one of the most important. In expanding and explaining this theme, Apple encourages designers to consider the app's functionality first and then to think about whether or not a feature is absolutely relevant to the app's overall function. If not, it's probably best to leave it out.

Next, make sure that your app's design adapts to the various devices in the ecosystem so that users are able to experience your app, regardless of the device they happen to use. The experience should be tailored to each device.

This can be seen as a tall order until you realize that there are plenty of examples to follow in Apple's own apps. Apple's apps run the gamut from utilities to tools and productivity, so you should be able to find something that suits your need, illustrates a principle, or shows a UI element that you are thinking about using. If you don't find Apple's stock list of applications that come preinstalled with any iOS device helpful, it is also a good idea to check out the recommended apps in the Apple App Store, as shown in Figure 5-1. These provide great examples of design, which either adhere strictly to Apple's design principles or innovate beautifully on the existing paradigms.

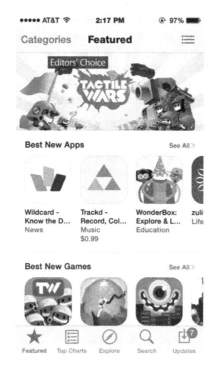

Figure 5-1. *The Apple App Store often showcases apps that are best-in-class examples of their design principles or that are doing a great job of innovating based on those principles*

When designing your app, you also want to let your content take precedence over anything else on the screen. Essentially, this means that the design of your User Interface should be so seamless that the user barely notices it. Your content should shine and use the entire screen as its canvas, with the most important information taking standing out above everything else—including the UI. In fact, the HIGs state explicitly that the UI should play a "supporting role" to everything else on the screen.

If you're planning on using the very popular Gaussian Blur (discussed in Chapter 3), take the approach of using the blur and transparency to orient the user further to what is happening on the screen and to provide the overall context to where elements will live on the screen. Translucency will let users know that there are additional elements behind a panel, and the blur can be used to add some context to the overall design.

Clarity

Clarity is extremely important when designing for mobile devices. Because of the limited screen space, designers are pressed to put many different options onto a very small screen while still being clear and user friendly. It is quite the challenge. However, to assist those designing for iOS with this challenge, Apple has elevated the need for clarity above some other design principles.

Clarity in design centers around the way that elements are laid out on the screen in relation to each other so that a user can interact with the app successfully. If you have done your job correctly, then upon first viewing a screen or page in your app, the user will have an instinctive feel as to how to relate to the elements they see before them. If a user has to try too hard or too long to understand what and how the elements relate to each other, then they will lose interest and you will likely lose them as a user.

One of the ways that the HIGs state that designers can offer clarity in their designs is through the use of negative space. Negative space is an important design element. Quite simply, *negative space* translates in to "nothing" or even white space in a design. It is space that is not filled with a design element or even content. Great designers use negative space to their advantage. Sometimes, designers, especially those who aren't as experienced, tend to think it is necessary to fill all of the space on a screen with *something.* This is far from the case. A key characteristic of negative space is that it helps to keep the user's focus on the object as opposed to what is around it. The negative space helps to focus the user's attention.

Negative space is a tool that is used fairly frequently in logo designs. Graphic designers will use the negative space in words or in a logo to call attention to a shape of some sort. But negative space can be used in website design to balance content as well as in app designs. Using negative space in your app designs helps to highlight the content further and guides the user to where you want them to go in your app.

The HIGs use the iMessages app as a great example of the use of negative space in iOS design. This is an excellent example because here the negative space enhances readability. Since the iMessages app consists mainly of words on a screen, it is important to make sure that the content is readable and clear to the users of the apps and persons in a conversation.

Let's take a closer look at the iMessages app. Figure 5-2 shows a conversation between two people. Those of us who are familiar with the iPhone and iMessages will recognize it as a conversation where both individuals are on iOS. In the conversation, the blue bubble represents your messages and the gray bubble represents the recipient's. If the person on the other end is not on iOS, the conversations appear as green and white text bubbles. Note how the text bubbles appear on either side of the screen to create a balance and to show the "flow of the conversation." By leaving space on either side of the screen, the user's eyes will follow the conversation naturally. This is the effect of using negative space in your app designs. Imagine the effect if the text bubbles were in-line and on the same side of the screen as opposed to on opposite sides of the screen.

Figure 5-2. *Use of negative space in the iMessages app*

Apple is known for its use of negative space, and so it would be expected that designers working to design apps for iOS also incorporate this use of negative space into their designs. Before you begin to design your app, think about how you can use negative space to improve readability, guiding users on a journey within a page or as they move throughout your app.

Negative space can even be used when working with spacing and margins, or even with photography. All of these elements on a screen and how they are placed in relation to each other will affect users and their ability to navigate within your app in addition to their overall experience.

Another tool that helps users relate to the content on the screen in your app is color. In fact, color is a powerful tool that helps users orient themselves to content and elements on the screen. You can use color to "speak" to your users by your design of your app. An entire book can be (and I'm sure has been) written on color and color theory in design. As we've already covered color specifically as it relates to Sketch, we won't dwell on it here. What we will briefly discuss is the use of color in your app designs, and as it pertains to designing for iOS.

The HIGs encourage designers to use color to provide visual cues to users of their apps. iOS specifically has system colors that are used throughout the built-in apps. For example, the Notes app features a fairly clean UI and uses a yellow color to highlight certain elements on the screen to guide users, as shown in Figure 5-3.

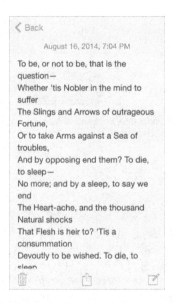

Figure 5-3. The Notes app and its use of a highlight color to help orient users to the UI

The HIGs encourage designers first to create a color palette for their app that consists of colors that complement each other, but that also look great against both light and dark backgrounds. It is also important for designers to make sure that they check their colors at various times of the day to ensure that each color (especially ones with custom tints) are viewable even in the harshest, sunniest conditions, or on the cloudiest of days.

Depth

The last theme that Apple set forth for designers working on iOS apps is *depth*. Depth is something that really came through with the redesign of the operating system with iOS7 and has been a part of the look and feel of iOS ever since. It added much-needed layers and richness to the experience of interacting with iPhone and iPad screens. Depth in design is an interesting concept because it asks designers to add another dimension to a traditionally two-dimensional experience.

One of the ways to bring a sense of depth to your iPhone designs is to have overlapping objects. Whenever there are overlapping objects on a screen, you are creating a sense of depth for your users. How you do this is up to you. As with other design themes for iOS, you can take cues from the built-in apps. And even with the advent and popularity of "Flat Design," depth is still a desired design element in apps.

When done correctly, depth will add a very clear visual hierarchy to your designs, and it purposefully orients users to the content on the screen. For example, once an app on the iPhone or iPad's home screen is placed in a folder, accessing that folder brings up a window that shares the same background as the screen so that the user is always aware that they are in the home screen environment. The title of the folder appears at the top of the page to provide additional context. This layout is shown in Figure 5-4.

Figure 5-4. An app folder on the iPhone's home screen in iOS8 shows how depth is a natural part of the iOS design ecosystem

Devices and Resolutions

Before you start designing your app, you will need to consider where your app will reside and what devices will be best to run your software. The number of mobile devices running iOS has increased since its initial release in 2007. Today, designers must consider all of the various devices in Apple's product line before they begin to design their apps. Sketch does offer templates of different sizes to get you started quickly with designing your app, but it's a good idea to have a sense not only of the different devices, but of their resolutions as well.

With each new release and update of the iOS operating system, Apple will occasionally deprecate older versions of the iPhone. With iOS8, the earliest supported device is now the iPhone 4S. This is not to say that the OS won't perform on older phones, just that it won't perform optimally. With iOS9's release, the list of compatible devices changes somewhat. All of the currently supported iOS devices are shown in Figure 5-5.

Figure 5-5. List of all compatible devices for iOS9

These then represent the entire suite of devices upon which your app will operate when it is released. It is important to think about the different ways in which users interact with these devices and thus how they will interact with your app as well. For example, many iPad owners use the devices as a replacement for their desktop computers or laptops, while the iPhone is a more personal device and is often used on the go or while in transit. These are all conditions that will influence how and when users interact with your app.

In recent years, as more devices have been released, the resolution of the devices has also increased, offering bigger, clearer, and crisper screens to view content. The very first iPhone released had a resolution of 320 × 480 pixels. However, when the iPhone 4S was released, it included a Retina screen. Thus while it had the exact same screen *dimensions*, its resolution was 640 × 960 pixels, roughly double that of the previous model. If you take the concept of squares-to-pixels as 1:1, a Retina screen has double the number of pixels in the same space. As way of comparison, the newly released iPhone 6 Plus has a Retina HD resolution of 1920 × 1080 pixels on its 5.5-inch screen. The screen resolutions of the iPhone 6 models are illustrated in Figure 5-6. When you consider all of the elements that we talked about earlier like color, deference, negative space, and clarity, you must consider that the level of detail on screens has also increased significantly.

iPhone 6

4.7"
RETINA HD DISPLAY

1334
×750
RESOLUTION: 326 PPI

iPhone 6 Plus

5.5"
RETINA HD DISPLAY

1920×
1080
RESOLUTION: 401 PPI

Figure 5-6. *The screen resolutions and display sizes of the iPhone 6 and iPhone 6 Plus*

With multiple devices on the market and multiple resolutions to consider for your designs, you will still want to create pixel-perfect designs that look great regardless of which device your user chooses. It's important to understand the difference between points and pixels. Pixels are actually small squares that make up the shapes in your designs. For designers working with multiple screen sizes and resolutions, sharpness is important. If your designs are not crisp, the imperfections will show up—especially on higher-resolution screens—and they will appear blurry.

Some designers will typically design for 1× and then scale up to accommodate higher resolutions. Others will design at 2× and then scale down to 1× from there. If you start your designs at 2×, it is always a good idea to use pair numbers, which will help you avoid issues if you must scale down to 1×.

If you are designing and the numbers of pixels in your design are not even pairs, you will run into issues when you attempt to export your work and also when you attempt to scale it for a new resolution. Here's why: When designing for higher-resolution screens, the number of pixels increases exponentially. This can cause complications not only in design but in development for iOS. Therefore, Apple introduced the *point* system when it introduced the Retina screen with the iPhone 4S. To understand this better, think about the following example. The iPhone 4S and the iPhone 3G had the same physical dimensions. However, because of the introduction of the Retina screen, the resolution of the 4S essentially quadrupled the resolution of the screen while its dimensions remained the same. This is because Apple increased the number of pixels in a *point*. Previously, 1 point = 1 pixel. With the advent of the Retina screen, 1 point = 4 pixels. The point system makes developing for Retina screens easier.

Thus if you have an image that measures 100 × 100 pixels, it will render at 100 × 100 pixels on a standard non-Retina screen. However, the same image on a Retina screen will render at 100 × 100 pixels, but it will look half the size. This is because the Retina screen renders the image at an increased pixel density. However, using the point system, the same 100 × 100 pixel image will now render @2× the size on a Retina screen in order to normalize what the user sees.

In Xcode, everything is measured in points. However, in Sketch 3, everything is measured in pixels. For those who are aiming for pixel perfection in their designs, the number of devices and resolutions can sometimes be tricky. Designers are now possibly designing for three different resolutions: @1× (iPhone 3), @2× (iPhone 5 and iPhone 6), and @3× (iPhone 6 Plus).

Sketch has included a feature called Round to the Nearest Pixel Edge. If your shapes do not use pairs, but use decimals or half-pixels instead, using this feature will help you to trim the dimensions of your design to the nearest pair value so that your exports and scaling can be seamless.

Figure 5-7 shows how this works. The figure shows an image on the Sketch canvas. Note that the dimensions in the Inspector on the right are not paired. In fact, these dimensions include decimals. Assuming that the images are already @2×, the decimals will make it difficult to scale the image down to @1× because the dimensions will need to be divided yet again. This division will result in a new image that does not maintain the crispness of the original even-numbered design when exported for different resolutions. By using the Round to the Nearest Pixel Edge feature, you will see that the dimensions are rounded to whole numbers that are easily divisible to round up or down to additional resolutions.

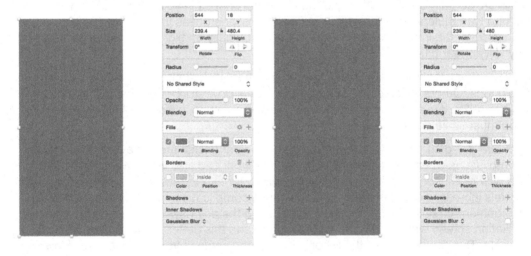

Figure 5-7. Using the Round to the Nearest Pixel Edge feature in Sketch

Using Standard iOS Dimensions

We've already talked about using the templates that come with Sketch to begin designing your app, but did you also know that within those templates are standard elements that rarely ever change? You can make life easy for your developers once you hand over your Sketch files by keeping the standard elements within Apple's guidelines and also by keeping your app's UI as simple as possible. Since you will likely be using some of the elements from Sketch across difference artboards for different devices, let's talk about how to move them across various resolutions.

Upon opening the iOS template files, you will see that all of the iOS UI elements are symbols that have been created for your selection. While using these for simple mockups is great, a closer look will reveal that they were created @1× resolution, as shown in Figure 5-8.

This is a collection of symbols and text styles at 1x scale (375pt) for quickly mocking up iPhone apps, created by Bohemian Coding, and released under the MIT license

Figure 5-8. A note in the iOS UI Design Template in Sketch that lets users know that the symbols are created @1× (375pt) for designs

This means that some adjusting will be necessary when using these standard elements in your designs for additional resolutions (@2× and @3×). If you attempt to scale the elements as is, you'll notice that some shifting of the elements as a whole, as well as the individual elements that make up the symbols, will be needed. To do this, they will need to be ungrouped first and then scaled—first to 200 percent and then to 300 percent if you are also designing for the iPhone 6 Plus. This applies to tab bars, status bars, and the like. Note that if you are simply creating mockups using Sketch, you can skip this exercise. However, if you are creating a design that will be used across multiple devices and sent to your developers, this is a good practice to include in your workflow. Figure 5-9 shows a standard UI status bar imported into artboards created for the iPhone 6 and iPhone 6 Plus.

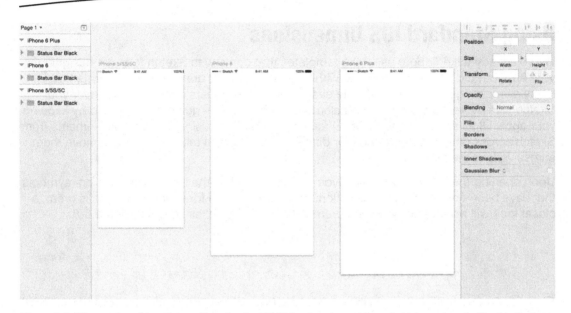

Figure 5-9. *Three artboard templates with a standard UI Status bar element imported into each and affixed to the top. No resizing has been done on the status bar*

Looking closely at Figure 5-9, you will see that the status bar is at 100 percent. When untouched and unscaled, it fits perfectly into the iPhone 6 artboard. This version of Sketch then assumes that an @1× is 375 × 667 pixel screen dimension, but since the actual resolution of the screen on the iPhone 6 is much higher, resizing and scaling the elements for each resolution will be necessary.

You should now be just about ready to start designing your app.

Summary

Every designer working to create apps for iOS will need to study and familiarize themselves with the HIGs, a set of documentation created and maintained by Apple to describe best practices for designers and developers. Though we've outlined the five main points as described by Apple for iOS design in this chapter, it's a good idea to refer back to this documentation often as you work with the platform.

In the next chapter, we will discuss how to set your design preferences to optimize your workflow. You'll see how doing this before starting your designs will make it easier on you, and how it will streamline your design process.

Optimizing Your Workflow

If you are reading this book, you are probably new to Sketch and are either new to design, or coming to it from another graphics program like Photoshop or maybe even Fireworks. If you're coming from another design program, you will want to check out this chapter because in it, I will share with you some great tips for optimizing your workflow.

Typically, with graphics programs, optimizing your workflow will involve you computer's hardware setup, setting preferences, saving and recovery of files, and increasing the overall performance of the program. But workflow also involves doing the little things that will help to save the most important commodity that there is—time.

If you're new to designing, you might still be figuring out what your workflow looks like. And, if you're new to Sketch, you might have heard or read that Sketch will help you to complete certain design tasks quickly and shave valuable minutes off your workflow. Even if you're an experienced designer, you will have an interest in saving time when creating your designs. This could be for your own personal reasons or because you need to please a client. When designing, time usually isn't your friend and the faster you can get your designs done, the better.

There are some well-known general tips, tricks, and strategies that you can use to speed up general tasks and there are some more specific ones that relate only to Sketch. In this chapter, we will focus initially on some general things you can do and then move onto some more Sketch-specific tips. We've already covered shortcuts back in Chapter X, so if you need to, you can add those to your list of things that you can do to speed things up. Once you are familiar with the list of shortcuts (we also cover how to create your own shortcuts), in addition to the tips in this chapter, you should be well on your way to speeding up your design process.

It's a good idea to mention, however, that while speed is great, it doesn't compare to quality. So make sure that you're balancing the two. No point in getting the work done quickly if it'll need to be redone. Better to get it done the right way first.

Customizing Your Workspace

Every design program will open with defaults intact. This means that there is a baseline for certain settings that are in place when you open a program on first launch. These are set as they are to hit the lowest common denominator for designers using the program. It is also a blank slate upon which you can then begin to set things up just as you would like. You will find that most design programs are easily customizable. This means, you can show and hide panels and windows to your choosing and depending on what projects you're working on and also what field you're working in. For example, if you're designing mainly user interfaces for app, your custom setup might be different from someone who is designing websites. Also, if you're designing for Android, your setup just might differ from the setup of someone who is designing primarily for iOS or even OS X.

You will likely be using certain tools and features more often than others and you can make sure that those tools are readily available to you without having to search for them. If you want to customize grids and rulers, you can easily do that so that you can set up your design to your liking as well.

You can always refer back to Chapter 2, where I describe how to customize your toolbar to keep the features of Sketch that you use the most readily available. As you can see in Figure 6-1, there's way more than meets the eye in the Sketch toolbar. The default shows icons and text but you can change this to show only icons or only text. You can also add or remove any or your favorite items to replace the ones in the default toolbar. This should probably be one of the first things you do to make Sketch your own. Set it up just the way you like and get off on the right foot with your work. Having frequently used icons right in the toolbar is always better than having them two or even three clicks away.

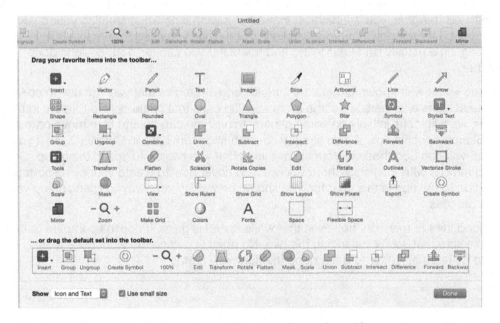

Figure 6-1. Sketch lets you customize the toolbar to add your most frequently used items and remove the ones you don't use as much

Preferences

Not everyone will appreciate the same default preferences that you find in graphics programs either. Therefore, most software designers and developers will create preferences that you can customize and change to your liking. Sketch does the same. Head over to the Sketch menu and click on Preferences to open up the Preferences panel. You can set preferences for your canvas and layers as well as some general preferences like font rendering and even how you want to set up your iOS device viewing in Sketch Mirror, as shown in Figure 6-2.

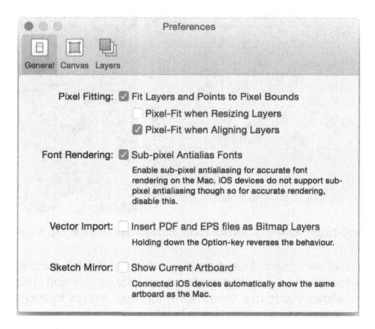

Figure 6-2. The Sketch Preferences panel allows you to add another layer of customization to your canvas

Organizing Your Document

If you are designing an app from start to finish, it is a good practice to think things through before you get to the design stage. Some designers use Sketch for wireframing but there are a number of tools currently on the market that allow you to wireframe and then import directly into Sketch. Others will use the old hand pen and paper to wireframe and iterate on an overall flow of the app before designing. Regardless of your approach, it is a good idea to think about how you will organize your document *before* you begin the design process. If you use pen and paper, you can easily take a photo of your drawing and import it directly into Sketch for reference. That way, you can use the drawing as a guide in the background of your designs, or side-by-side as a reference. Figure 6-3 shows how a paper drawing can be imported as an image into your design for reference.

Figure 6-3. You can import paper drawings or wireframes for reference into Sketch to help in the design process

With Sketch, you have the option of creating your entire app in ONE document or breaking it up into multiple documents depending on the complexity of your app. This is a game changer because it allows you to use Sketch's infinite zoom feature to zoom out and see your entire app at a bird's eye view. This is helpful as well when designing complex applications that have a number of different flows and use cases. While you can create one file for the entire app, Sketch allows you to break up your app into multiple pages so that you are able to share symbols across your entire document and thus your app should something change. Figure 6-4 shows a bird's eye view of all of the screens in my app Cast. While Cast is a simple app, you can easily use pages to split up the major sections of your app and then use the artboards within those pages to outline various steps in a specific process.

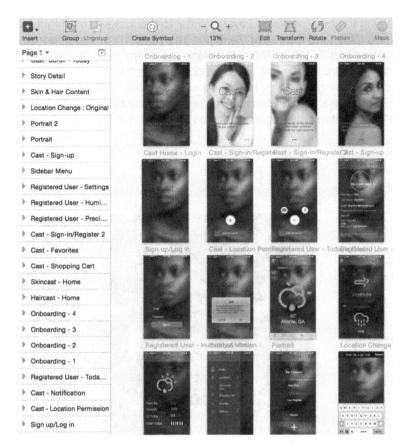

Figure 6-4. A bird's eye view of multiple screens of an app laid out on one page in Sketch

Flattening Images

This particular process speaks to making Sketch as fast and efficient as possible. Sketch is a pretty lean program anyway but graphics tend to slow anything down. As we all know, Sketch's strength isn't in handling photographs. It can, as we discussed in an earlier chapter, but because Sketch is a vector program, we recommend minimal use of photographs. That being said, you may still want to include photographs in your designs. Apps are visual and as such there will be some instances where they help to bring your app a level of realism. So, creating a way that we can work with images is helpful.

Because images contain significantly more information than natively created shapes do, they will require Sketch (and your computer) to use more resources when rendering them. Let's say for instance, you are using a background image that is quite prominent in your app. This will likely mean that the image is used on multiple screens. But let's complicate things by saying that there are also some effects that have been applied to that same layer. If you import the image, it's always a good idea to make sure that the overall size has been optimized to the lowest file size that will maintain the best level of quality. We know that the larger the file size, the better the image will appear. However, you must consider as well whether or not there will be special effects applied to the image. If, for example, you will be applying the ever-popular Gaussian Blur to the image, you might want to consider a lower quality (and thus size) file. Once you have the image imported, you can then apply the effect and flatten it. This will reduce the overall size of your Sketch document and ultimately the response speed of your computer while the document is open. Figure 6-5 shows two screens using the same background image with a blur effect and that has been flattened prior to use. While you may not see the immediate results of this unless your computer's RAM is frighteningly low, you will see the results in the overall file size of your document.

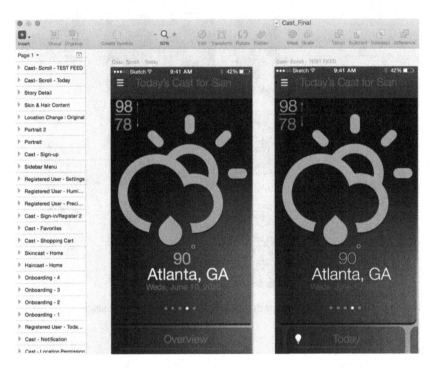

Figure 6-5. Two files with images as backgrounds, one optimized and one not

Naming Layers and Symbols

This is a tricky one. For me, naming layers can be a real pain. I move fast when designing and wireframing in Sketch. I often don't take the time to name layers as efficiently as I could. While it's not so bad when it comes to prototyping or wireframing, especially if it's just for your eyes, when you're designing a product that will be shared with other designers and ultimately with developers, you want to make sure that you are naming your layers and symbols in a way that is efficient but also intuitive for others who will be using your file(s). This is a hard-and-fast design rule regardless of what graphics program you are working in. It is a best practice to create names for layers that make sense. Being witty or obtuse is not advised.

If you haven't organized your layers and they start to become unwieldy, I'll provide some tips that will help you to manage them effectively. It is important to be able to organize your layers before you hand them off and even while you are working within your designs. The key is to organize your layers as you are designing *before* they get out of control.

We talked earlier about grouping items that are related to each other in your designs but sometimes, it's a good idea to group items for organization. For example, if you are designing an app with a tab bar, you might want to include all of the elements in that tab bar into one group. And, you can have a group within a group or nested groups as well where they make sense. So while your tab bar icons are in one group, if there is a group of shapes that make up a particular icon, then that can be a nested group within the larger tab bar group. This way, someone who will be working with your files can navigate to elements they need to get to without doing a ton of guesswork. Trust me, they will thank you for it. Figure 6-6 shows how I've organized my layers for the Cast Beauty app. The list shows major groups with their folders but each folder has a number of additional nested groups within and all relate to a singular artboard in that page.

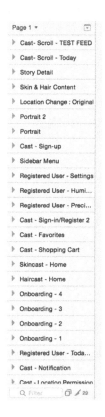

Figure 6-6. A list of named layers for an app

When it comes to symbols, you can bet that the same is true as with layers. Using symbols are the key to speeding up your work when there are changes to be made on the fly for clients or even creative directors. If you have a document that consists of 10 pages and you need to update the color of a header bar, sure you can make the change to every artboard or screen on every page of your app. Or you can name the symbol something intuitive like "header bar" and not "purple stripe" and easily change the color once and immediately have it update everywhere in the document. You do not want to waste time trying to find out where the correct symbol is because its name doesn't make sense. However, as with everything, be careful where you use them and how often. It's a good idea if you've changed symbols across your entire design to do a bit of design QA to make sure that the changes you've made are relevant and, more importantly, accurate.

Creating a Custom Grid

We've already covered the awesomeness that is Sketch's layout and grid settings. So, before you set about making the greatest app design ever, set up your layout settings by adjusting columns, width, and gutter settings. You can then you can set this up as your default by clicking the button shown in the lower left corner of Figure 6-7 so that you don't have to redo the process every time you start a new design.

Figure 6-7. The Layout Settings panel in Sketch. Use this to set up your canvas and save as default for quicker startups

Presentation Mode

Sometimes, it's important to view your work without any distractions. If you will need to show your work on your screen whether for your superiors, coworkers, or sometimes, even clients, then *Presentation Mode* is the way to go. By hitting the ⌘+. it will show your screen in presentation mode. This means that the menu bar, doc, and all extraneous items on the screen will disappear, leaving just your designs. You will be free to move around within the specific page. You can move through your artboards by scrolling up and down and left and right.

Tip   Hitting ⌘+ . will also get you out of Presentation mode.

Setting a Default Style

Whenever a shape is created in Sketch, it will always appear with Sketch's default style. Usually, shapes in Sketch appear with a light gray fill and a darker gray border. But, as with most things in Sketch, this can be easily changed. If you find that you are typically working in a particular color or with a color palette, you can always change this default color by creating a new style and setting it as the default. Say, for example that you want to have all new shapes appear in a specific shade of red fill with no border. First, you would create a red shape and change the fill color from the default gray to your specific shade of red. Then, you would remove the border setting, and last, you would navigate to Edit ➤ Set Style as default as shown in Figure 6-8. This will ensure that all newly created shapes will have the new default style as you've designated. This applies to any shape: circles, stars, triangles, etc.

> **Tip** One thing to note, however, is that styles like border radius, shadows, and reflections cannot be set as a default style.

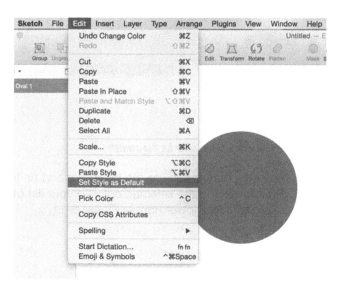

Figure 6-8. How to set a default style that will apply to all new shapes

Defining Your Color Palette

Before you actually begin to design your app you'll want to have chosen a specific color palette that you will use. This will include your main color, accent and highlight colors, and everything in between. There are some great tools available for selecting color palettes. Once you have selected a color palette, Sketch makes it easy to set this in the Inspector so that your colors remain easily accessible throughout the course of the project. You can get a screenshot of the palette from an online tool like Adobe's Kuler and import that into your Sketch canvas as shown in Figure 6-9.

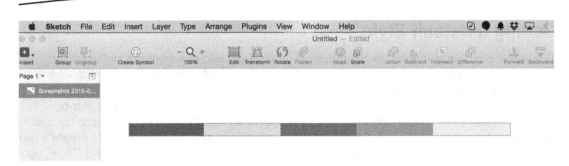

Figure 6-9. Series of colorful swatches imported into Sketch for the purpose of creating a color palette

Once the image has been imported, move your cursor to the dropper icon in the Inspector panel. Click the icon to reveal a magnifier that you can then move to the canvas and hover on the desired color in the image of the color palette as shown in Figure 6-10.

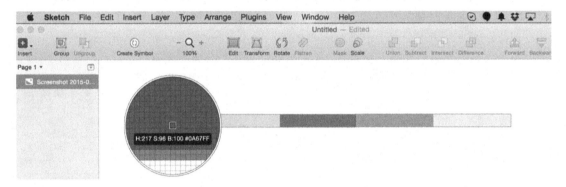

Figure 6-10. Dropper tool in Sketch that extracts the color for the swatch

Once you click that color, move the cursor back to the Inspector and hit the "+" button. Once you have done this, Sketch will add the selected color to your list of swatches in the area that reads "Document Colors" in the lower right in Figure 6-11.

Figure 6-11. New set of document colors created by using the dropper tool to copy the colors from the color palette image on the canvas

Having all colors of the palette easily accessible will save you time as you move through your design. And colors can be just as easily removed from the Inspector as they are added. To remove a color from the Inspector, simply click and drag it onto the canvas. Upon release, it will disappear in an animated cloud of smoke and be removed from the dock.

> **Tip**   Sketch can pull colors not only from your canvas but from anywhere in your screen including the desktop of your Mac or even a browser window.

The Rotation Tool

Sketch offers a little-known tool that can help you to save time in your designs. It's called the *Rotation Tool*, and while you may not use it often, as designers sometimes there is a need to create an effect that, if done by hand, can be incredibly time-consuming. You would need to evenly space every time on the path and ensure that they are all the same size as well as equidistant from each other. This is where the Rotation Tool comes in. Admittedly, I've not yet had to use this tool but I know it will come in handy at some point. To use this tool, you would create a shape on your canvas. This can be any shape in any color. For our example, we'll use a red circle. With the red circle created, navigate to the Layer menu and select Paths ➤ Rotate Copies as shown in Figure 6-12.

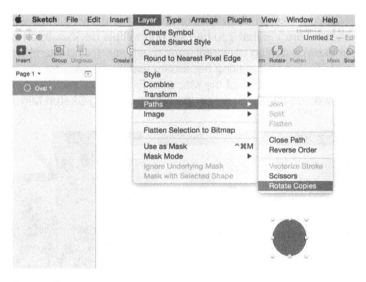

Figure 6-12. Access the Rotation Tool from the Layer menu

Once you've selected Rotate Copies, sketch will ask you how many copies you'd like to create. The default will be six and Sketch will tell you the total number of layers that will be generated once the task has been completed. The result of the number of copies you select and the layers are shown in Figure 6-13. Sketch has created multiple shapes along a round path, each in its own layer. The distance between each layer or shape can be altered by moving the handle attached to the original layer. Each shape can be moved closer together or further apart.

Figure 6-13. *The Rotation Tool will create multiples of the same graphic along a circular path quickly and seamlessly*

Sketch Mirror

While I briefly touched on the *Sketch Mirror* in Chapter 1, there is no mistaking that this feature is a huge time-saver when designing for iOS. Sketch Mirror is a companion app for the Sketch Mac app that allows you to preview your designs directly on a device while designing. Remember what this was like using another graphics program? You would usually have to export the image at the correct resolution, sending to yourself, and then opening it on the desired device for a preview. A bit tedious, indeed. Now, with Sketch Mirror, you can install the app on your iPhone or iPad, make sure that it is connected to the same Wi-Fi network as your computer, and be able to preview your designs right on the device. While viewing your designs, and depending on how your artboards have been set up, you can swipe between artboard and pages of your Sketch document on the device showing the preview. Another great thing about Sketch Mirror is that you can set up multiple devices upon which to view your designs. This makes designing universal apps much easier and seamless. Sketch Mirror makes the process of viewing and making necessary tweaks so easy for designers and its easily accessible right from the toolbar of the Mac app. Figure 6-14 shows an image of an artboard being previewed on the Mac and on the iPhone 6 using Sketch Mirror.

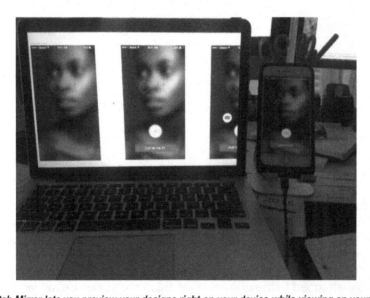

Figure 6-14. *Sketch Mirror lets you preview your designs right on your device while viewing on your Mac*

Other Workflow Tools

You will find that as a designer, you will eventually have to move outside of your preferred graphics program to interact with other members of your team. I'll cover a few of them below that I have personally used but you might find that your preference is for different programs, and that's fine. The goal here is to find the programs that complement your style and way of working so that you save time doing mundane things and spend more time doing what you love, which hopefully, is designing.

Flinto

Flinto is a prototyping tool that makes it easy to take all of your artboards, create links and interactions between them, and create a prototype. While there are quite a few prototyping tools, Flinto, I have found, is one of the easiest to use. As Sketch's artboards will already be in the correct size, Flinto makes it easy to see, understand, and create the relationships between each screen in your app. This way, there is a shift from just designing your app to really focusing on how the app works and the way that users will interact with it. Thus is the inevitable shift from UI to UX and important shift that many designers are dealing with at the moment.

Users simply have to import their screens into Flinto by dragging and dropping them or importing via Dropbox (the app offers easy Dropbox integration) into the Flinto canvas, as shown in Figure 6-15. Then, you add the desired connections and interactions between the screens and preview it either on your device or right on screen within the program. If something doesn't work, it's a quick fix to update the links or change the transition. To replace a screen, you can easily just drag the new screen on top of the old one and Flinto will automatically update it.

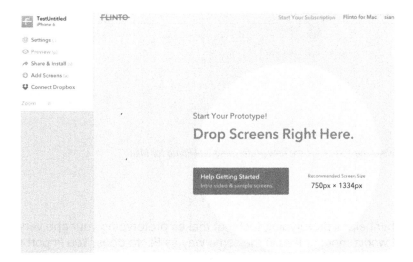

Figure 6-15. The Flinto interface is easy to use and lets you drag and drop screens into the interface

Flinto will emulate some standard iOS transitions as well and you can easily add a Back button to most pages. And you can even add a starter image and app icon so that your users have a real app experience.

When you're all done, you can email your prototype to potential users or even send as a text message. As you continue to iterate on your app, your users will automatically view the updated version of the app, and if for any reason you need to revoke access to the app, that's a pretty simple process, too. There are quite a few prototyping tools on the market, but Flinto is definitely one of the easiest to use and my favorite.

Flinto for Mac

The team at Flinto has recently released Flinto for Mac, a prototyping app for OS X that allows designers to create simply or more comprehensive prototypes with more complicated interactions. While I haven't tried Flinto for Mac personally as it's virtually brand new at the time of this writing, it's been given great reviews by designers I trust and respect. It allows you to create a series of complex animations with no programming and within an interface that's just as intuitive and as easy to use as the Flinto Web app (see Figure 6-16). You can drag and drop assets from any graphics program, or use the Sketch plug-in that will let you automatically import your designs from Sketch and right into Flinto for Mac. The app also allows you preview on a device so that you can test out your transitions on an app as well.

Figure 6-16. The welcome screen for the new prototyping tool Flinto for Mac

Marvel

Marvel is another helpful prototyping tool that makes prototyping your app very easy (see Figure 6-17). It works more or less in the same way as Flinto does. You import your screens into Marvel using Dropbox, add hotspots, links, and transitions, and then test. Once you're ready to share your prototype with others, you can send via e-mail (unique URL), text, QR code, or you can even embed the prototype directly into your website. These days, designers are encouraged to iterate and test often. With these prototyping tools, the job becomes that much easier and allows you to make the needed changes without committing any code at all. It's also worth noting that Marvel also has a mobile app that brings some of the functionality offered in the Web app to your iPhone. You actually take pictures of the sketches that you've created and link them together right within the app.

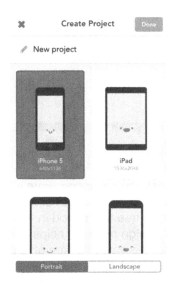

Figure 6-17. Screen from the Marvel mobile app that lets you create prototypes on the fly

Dropbox

Last but not at all least in the workflow sections is Dropbox, the popular cloud storage tool. While Dropbox is not at all design-only tool, it is a valuable tool for designers to be able to not only store, but share their designs with the world. As you may have already noted as well, some of the prototyping tools that I've already mentioned here in this section were either built on the Dropbox API or uses it or authentication. This means that if you already use Dropbox to store your designs, you can easily import them into either Flinto or Marvel to speed up your workflow and allow you to focus less on file sizes and types and more on the quality of your work. With Flinto, you can store all of your images in Dropbox and Flinto keeps them in synch if you happen to make changes or updates to them. Both programs ask for access to your Dropbox account in order to maintain this feature. Flinto will ask to connect your Dropbox account, as shown in Figure 6-18.

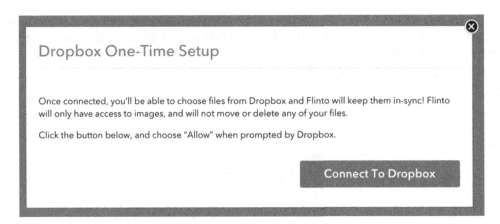

Figure 6-18. Dropbox One-Time Setup window

These are just some of the tools that you can incorporate into your workflow as you work on your app in Sketch. Some you will like more than others. What's really important is to try a few out. Most of these apps have a free trial period in which you can experiment and see what works best for you and your design needs. If helps to try specific tasks and see where you can save time. If something shaves valuable time off a process or task then keep it. Also, explore ways in which you can customize these programs further to suit your needs. When it comes to some of these programs, customization is key, as with Sketch.

InVision

InVision is a Web-based prototyping tool that has become quite popular with designers. It's great for collaboration with large teams when there are many people who need to weigh in on designs quickly. This includes clients, other designers, project managers, or just the team at large. InVision lets you collect feedback from within the interface, and it allows you to track multiple versions of your design accurately, which can be an issue when working with large teams. The interface, as shown in Figure 6-19, is fairly simple, and you can sign up for free to try it out with one design. Additional designs are available, depending on your needs, for a monthly fee.

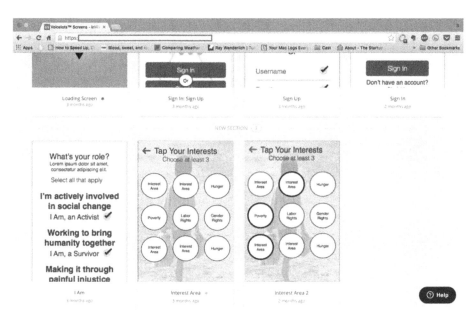

Figure 6-19. InVision interface

Summary

Everything listed in this chapter is optional. However, the more that you design, the more you will come to know that speed and efficiency are a keys to becoming a great designer—especially when you're dealing with clients and a team. Tips like setting preferences, getting your color palette just right, and setting up your document will go a long way to making you a fast and efficient designer.

But Sketch is just one program. The other programs mentioned in this chapter are included to help augment what Sketch can do. Many of them are available on a trial basis, so you can try them out for free until you find one that you wish to purchase.

In the next chapter, we'll discuss how to begin wireframing your app with Sketch and the tools listed previously. Then you should be ready to dive right in.

Chapter 7

Wireframing Your App with Sketch

As you may already know, wireframing is a great way to map out what your app will do and how it will do it before we move into the design stage. Wireframes are the blueprint of your app. They are often devoid of color or styling and you can focus on the basics of what your app will do before you add beautiful colors and effects we discussed earlier. When you wireframe your app, your goal is to focus on the functionality and details of how the user will interact with all the screens in your app.

If your app is fairly simple, you might be able to get away with not wireframing your app at all. But, I recommend always going through the wireframing process. It helps to clarify functionality in the early stages and gives you a clear understanding of how your app will behave once it's built. There are numerous tools available for wireframing: Balsamiq, MockFlow, UXPin, Omnigraffle, and Axure, to name a few. They range in cost from totally free to a few hundred dollars for a single license. If you've been using a particular tool to wireframe out your apps and it works well for your workflow, then I encourage you to stick with it. But if you're looking for a new tool that will help to speed up the overall process, then I encourage you to look no further than Sketch 3. Since we'll be designing our app in Sketch anyway, why not use it to wireframe your app as well? Many of the processes we've learned thus far in the previous chapters are well suited for not only designing but also for your wireframes.

There are some who believe that the process of wireframing should be very simple and quick. I am not one of those people. I believe that wireframing above all, should be thorough. If that takes one hour or five days, then so be it. In the end, you will have immersed yourself in the process of creating your app and will also be the person most qualified and able to design it. Wireframing is where you really get to understand the app you are about to design, so I think that this process can be short or long but more importantly it should be complete and should never be rushed as this will inevitably lead to issues later on in the design and build phases of your project. You will be exploring where elements in your app fit on the screen to be accessed by a user, so spending this time to get to understand that UI is critical. Therefore, if you take some much-needed extra time to complete your wireframes, that's perfectly fine.

In this chapter we will briefly discuss various techniques and processes for using Sketch to create your wireframes. We already discussed that Sketch has a thriving community and there are now quite a few websites that have been set up for the sole purpose of providing Sketch resources. We will list them later on in this book but for the purpose of wireframing you can do a simple search on Google for Sketch wireframing tools to see what's out there. You'll find that there are wireframing templates galore and you should be able to find one that suits your needs.

If you, like me, lean towards low-fidelity wires with very little or no branding, you might want to try to download one of the many templates that offer a sparse look and feel and that allow you to focus on the user experience as much as possible. It's also a good idea to try to find a template that will take advantages of some of Sketch's awesome features that will greatly improve your workflow. For example, Sketch guru Meng To has a few wireframing templates on his site that are fairly monochrome and use subtle shades of blue and gray. They are pretty good looking, are free to download, and are Sketch files that you can import right into your canvas and begin to work.

> **Tip** Meng To's site has great Sketch tips: `http://blog.mengto.com/`.

One of the great things about Meng's wireframing templates is that he's a Sketch master and goes out of his way to ensure that his templates contain iOS elements in dimensions that are completely in line with the iOS guidelines. The templates also utilize linked styles that are great because you can easily update the colors to suit your taste and update the entire wireframe easily.

Of course you can also create your own wireframes for your app by simply using the included iOS template that comes with Sketch or your trusty pen and paper to help with the process. For those who prefer to use pen and paper, you can use UI Stencils, a set of iPhone and iPad stencil kits that contain many popular UI elements for iOS. They also offer a line of notepads with the outline of the iPad and iPhones that make it easy to get started on your wireframing process. While not absolutely necessary, the stencils do add a layer of polish to regular old pen-and-paper wires. The tools are shown in Figure 7-1. Once you've crated your wires in pen and paper you can import them into Sketch to aid with the overall design process. But for now, let's focus on actually creating your designs in Sketch.

Figure 7-1. Wireframe templates in grays and blues from Meng To's website

The App

For the purposes of this exercise, we've decided to create a few key screens of a fictional app called PhotoBomb. The app lets users take photographs tagged with geolocation information on a map of landmarks or specific locations. Users can view their friends' photos and see what they did at that particular location. The app will use the user's location and their camera. The users will also sign in using either their Facebook or Twitter accounts. We will be creating a few key screens of the wireframes for this app using Sketch. I have already made preliminary sketches in my notepad with pencil. I've made notes in terms of the app's functionality, what the UI could potentially look like, and some other elements that are critical to the overall functionality of the app.

FROM MY NOTES

The app is meant to be simple to use and fun, combining elements of popular social networking sites like Facebook and Twitter. The order of our wireframes will be as follows:

The app will launch with a brief splash or intro screen containing the logo and introduction to the app. The user will click an "Enter" button that will take them to some onboarding screens that explain how the app works and how the user is meant to move through the various pages of the app. Users may skip the onboarding screens at any time and get right to the registration and authentication pages.

A user can register via one of three ways: Facebook, Twitter, or e-mail. I've decided to show only the e-mail authentication pages in our wireframes. Users enter the standard e-mail and password combination and then move onto the home page. This is the main page in the app where the user will arrive upon entry into the app. Users navigate from and to all other pages in the app from here. With this page completed, we'll show an example of the settings page for the app where users can adjust location and privacy settings, show a quick example of what the user's profile page will look like, and then move onto the permissions and capture pages which will show custom pages for getting a user's permission to use their camera and location. The last page we will wireframe will be a simple capture page that will illustrate our custom camera capture screen.

The notes I've written out by hand are shown in Figure 7-2. Notes can be added to your wireframes as annotations where necessary to explain intended actions for your designer or your engineering team.

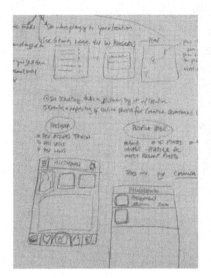 

Figure 7-2. My notes for the PhotoBomb app. I will use these to create my wireframes and will add annotations where necessary

I will refer to my pen-and-paper sketches and notes throughout the creation of my wireframes and use them as a guide to help me check on the screens and placement of specific elements, buttons, and icons along the way. If you don't have a document like this, it's a good idea to create one before you even begin your wireframes. You can call it your preliminary app spec and this will be a living document that will guide you through the creation of your wireframes.

We will create a few specific screens from our PhotoBomb app to show you how to create wireframes before moving to the design phase.

The Splash Screen

To create our splash screen, arguably the easiest screen in the app, we only really need the logo and placement of the title and name of the app. Using Meng's wireframe template, I duplicated an empty screen and created a new Sketch file called PhotoBomb. I then copied a blank screen from the template into the new file. This will become the splash screen of my app. Our splash screen will only have our logo and the name of the app on it. Human Interface Guidelines stipulate that the splash screen is only really on the screen for a short period of time. We plan to mitigate this by adding a button for registration and entry into the app.

With the blank screen I typed the word and imported the graphic for effect to create the logo. Then I used a rounded rectangle shape with no fill to create the button. That's the first screen as shown in Figure 7-3. Note that as we have learned earlier, I've started to name my layers appropriately and group elements just in case something needs to be updated on the fly later. All of the elements on the screen have been grouped to prevent confusion and for easy access.

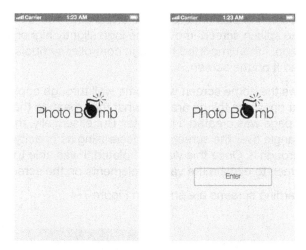

Figure 7-3. *The splash screen and enter screen of our Photo Bomb app wireframes*

With our splash screen created, we can now move onto a new screen where users will make a choice around how they choose to authenticate and use the app.

Onboarding

Onboarding is a new-ish practice that essentially consists of a including a few screens loaded before the user enters into the app that offers them—especially first-time users to understand the app and to demonstrate to them how the application will work. Arguably, some apps do not need onboarding screens or walkthroughs. If your app is relatively simple, then you can choose to ignore onboading screens altogether. However, if your app includes a unique way of handling a task that may not be immediately apparent to users, or if your app includes new user interface elements that users won't be familiar with, then you should consider including a few onboarding screens.

Onboarding screens are sometimes called walkthroughs. They are specifically used to familiarize users with a unique or completely new interaction that your app features. In these cases, walkthroughs are used to show users precisely how to interact with the more unique aspects of your app. When offering users onboarding or walkthrough screens, remember that it's important to show them as opposed to tell them and make sure that you're showing the entire process. Users want to know how to complete specific critical tasks in the app so be sure to show them all screens involved in that process. They also want to understand what your app will do for them. Meaning, what is the overall value proposition of your application?

And while visuals are important in your onboarding and walkthrough screens, it's important to ensure that the voice and tone you are using is friendly, conversational, and aligns with the rest of the copy in your app. Because these screens will be your user's very first interaction with your app, they will often determine whether or not your users will continue with the process of registration and continue their engagement with your app. If you're going to do onboarding, you've got to do it right. For our PhotoBomb app, we will include a few onboarding screens that explain the purpose of the app and what users can expect from it.

The initial onboarding screen explains the purpose of the app. This screen was created by taking a duplicate of the splash screen, moving the logo slightly higher, and adding a block of text describing the app. I then imported the page controller symbols from Sketch's iOS template and positioned it on the screen.

The second page shows the home screen with some walkthrough copy overlaid to provide a user with some context on where things are and what they mean to the overall game play. I'll explain how the home page was created a little later. But essentially, this screen was created by adding a black rectangle over the screen and decreasing its opacity to allow the page underneath to show through it. Once this was completed, I was able to add the copy as new layers on top of the screen to explain the various elements on the screen.

The two screens onboarding screens are shown in Figure 7-4.

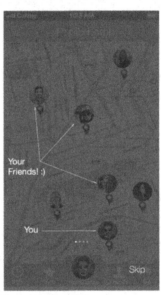

Figure 7-4. Two onboarding wireframed screens for our PhotoBomb app. On the left is the screen that explains the value proposition of the app, and on the right is a basic overlay showing placement of certain elements on the home page

Authentication

Most apps will require some kind of authentication for users to be able to enter and use the app's services. These days, some apps find it easier to use popular social networks that most users are members of. It makes the registration process easier. Since social networks already authenticate users, registering with their APIs, and most users are familiar with this process, they only need to choose the appropriate social network that they want to use for authentication. If they choose to, they can also register using e-mail. It is rarely necessary to wireframe the social media registration process, so we will create two pages, one where users can select which social media they want to register with, and another where they go through the process via e-mail registration.

We create the first page by duplicating the background and status bar from the previous page. We now have a blank screen upon which to build our new page. The new page must contain the three buttons for registration as well as the logo for the app. Figure 7-5 shows the newly created page.

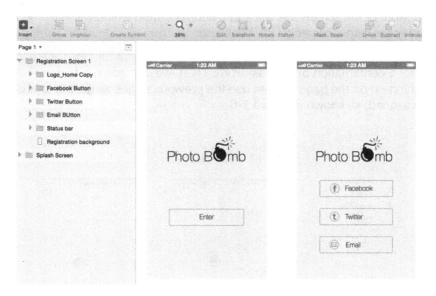

Figure 7-5. New registration page with buttons for social media and e-mail registration

To keep everything consistent in terms of size I have duplicated the button from the splash page three times to create one each for Facebook, Twitter, and e-mail buttons and then import the icons for each button as PNGs from a free icons set from Pixel Love. After resizing them and lining them up, we have our new page. Sitting next to our original page, the two aren't looking so bad and our wireframes are coming along. We now have two pages and can move on to the next page of our authentication process. You may want to know why I chose not to lay out the individual Facebook and Twitter authentication processes. It is mainly because those screens are mostly controlled by their respective publishers and designers have minimal control over how they will look. The apps require you to authenticate with those social media services and then return to your app so the popup screens for those services won't require much or any real design or layout decision making from us. Therefore, I'll choose to only show the e-mail authentication process, and show a few screens in the next section.

Tip   Pixel Love icons can be found at: **http://www.pixellove.com/free-icons**.

E-mail Registration

The next page I will create will be the e-mail registration page. Once the user has opted to register for our app using e-mail authentication, the app will now ask users to enter a username, an e-mail address, and a password with which they will enter the application. At the very bottom of the screen, we will add a submit button which will initiation the registration process with a server on the back end.

We will need to create three fields on this page: one for a username, one for a password, and another for a confirmation of the password. Then, we can add our button. Taking care to line everything up on the page we can use the previous pages as guides to ensure that all elements are aligned, as shown in Figure 7-6.

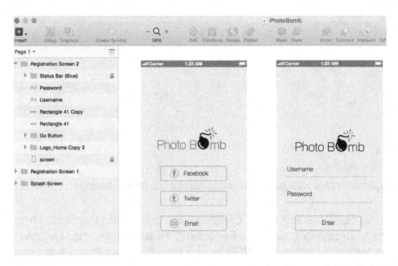

Figure 7-6. *Second registration screen with input fields for a username, password, confirmation of password, and an Enter button*

It is sometimes customary when creating wireframes to also create an alternate screen that shows how the elements on the screen will shift once the keyboard has been introduced onto the screen and a user is entering information. When wireframing it's a good idea to show as many views as possible so that there are no questions on placement of content on your screen.

Figure 7-7 shows the PhotoBomb sign-in screen with the raised keyboard and the cursor where the user will begin to type their username. The idea is that the contents of the page and associated fields will shift up with the introduction of the keyboard. It's a good idea for first-time designers to discuss this functionality with the engineer, as it's quite common to see keyboards covering text fields in new designs.

Figure 7-7. PhotoBomb sign-in screen with the keyboard and cursor as a guide for your developers

With e-mail registration, typically, a user is asked to verify their identity when an e-mail is sent to the e-mail address they've used to register within the app. After authentication, they are brought back into the app to complete the process. Typically, it is expected that users will verify their e-mail directly from their mobile device, so the process is relatively seamless.

Home Page

Now that our users have registered for the app and their identities have been confirmed, they are in the app. The home page of the app is the first page they see after registration and is also the page they will return to every time they open the PhotoBomb app. Therefore, the elements on this screen are more important than almost any other page in our app. This page must follow through on the promise of the app. Whatever it was that made the user download your app is what they will expect on this screen. It must orient them to the entire purpose of your app in a very short amount of time. The page must also contain navigational elements so that the user is able to navigate to other pages of your app from here and if need be, return at any time. In thinking about this page, I will refer back to my notes from Figure 7-2 as a reference. It will help to remind me what the overall purpose of the app is and keep that top of mind so that I can ensure that everything on the page is accessible and easy to find. This is where the main task of the app is to be located.

Once we've referenced our list we have decided to take a straightforward approach to the design of this page. The page will have, as a location-based app, a map on this main screen as well as a tab bar across the bottom to take users to the other areas of the app. Also on this page are areas where the user can see other locations that users near them have "bombed" or tagged other photographs. The user can also see profile pictures of each user so that they are easily recognizable.

In Figure 7-8 we have the basic wireframe of the home page. As with wireframes, the icons are for placement only and to give a very basic representation of where elements go on the screen. The page was created by importing some royalty-free images from Death to Stockphotos and icons from Pixel Love. The icons in the tab bar are a part of the wireframing template; we simply changed the titles associated with each icon.

Figure 7-8. Wireframe of the home page of the PhotoBomb app

Our map pin icons were randomly found by doing a search on the Internet, and the map background was imported from our iOS Design Template included with Sketch.

Preferences Page

Not all apps these days have a preferences page. If your app is fairly simple, then it makes sense not to have one. You can probably get away with just the basic settings included in iOS's Settings app that allow you to cover things like general privacy and notifications. An example of the standard iOS Settings page as well as the settings section of the Apple Store app this is shown in Figure 7-9.

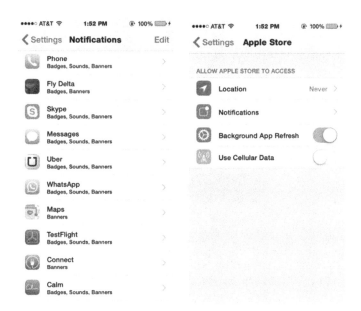

Figure 7-9. The Settings section on any iOS device provides users with a degree of control over their apps and the device in general

For our app, however, I've made a list of additional preferences that a user might want to be able to adjust. These would fall outside of the typical settings such as notifications and privacy. For example, a user may want to set the radius of the available photos that they can see at any given time. For areas with not many players to the game, a user might want to broaden that area to see more photos and to also play with more people. Alternately, for dense city areas, a user might want more control over the radius.

In some instances, a user might want to be able to prevent certain users from seeing their images. Our preferences will allow them to be able to add a "Block List" of players who are restricted from seeing their photos or from playing the game with them altogether. When it comes to privacy, users are very particular, so we have opted to increase the level of control a user can implement while playing the Photo Bomb game.

The preferences page was created by using a simple table view from our wireframe template as well as the disclosure indicators for each cell. I changed the colors to match our wireframe template and added the headings for each subsequent page that I retrieved from my notes and then included them in each cell in the table view. The first level of our preferences page is now complete and shown in Figure 7-10.

Figure 7-10. PhotoBomb first level of the Settings section of the PhotoBomb app

With the preferences page in the app, we will also need to consider whether each option brings up a new page or happens within the preferences environment. We must also consider how a user navigates back to the home page. In this instance, it is important to refer back to your human interface guidelines to understand navigational conventions for iOS.

Profile Page

If a user has to register for an app and select a photo from his or her camera roll for their profile picture, it's usually a good idea to add a profile page to your app. This way, a user can make changes to their profile whenever they choose to. Sometimes a profile page is editable from within the Settings page and sometimes it isn't. I thought it would be worth showing what the PhotoBomb user profile page would look like, since as a mobile design pattern, there are a number of different ways that this page can look. I decided to keep the profile page as simple as possible but a quick wireframe of what the page looks like will be helpful once we move into the design phase of the app.

The profile page is a common design pattern, and a quick search of popular design pattern sites like Pttrns, Mobile Patterns, or Inspired UI will reveal a number of different ways to present this information. Most do, however, have a few things in common, like a user photo and other information that is pertinent to the app like followers, likes, places visited, friends, and so forth. Take a look and determine which is best for you, or create your own. Remember, however, that a profile page should provide more information on the user than you can provide elsewhere in the app.

This page was created by starting out with another blank screen duplicated from one of our earlier screens. The idea for this page is that the user arrives here after hitting the Edit Profile cell in the previous page's wireframe. Once here, the user can tap the Edit button to make any changes.

I imported the user's image from the home page and made it slightly larger and centering it. Using text blocks in various sizes creates the rest of the page to round out the wireframe of the Profile page shown in Figure 7-11.

Figure 7-11. PhotoBomb profile page

Permissions

Getting your user's permission to use certain services and features on their phone is required by iOS. Users must explicitly give permission to allow third-party apps and software access to their microphone, camera, contact list, and location, among others. The way that software developers typically request this information has evolved over the years. Initially, a small notification asking for permission would pop up on a user's screen. The user would then allow or deny the service from being used by the app. An example of a typical permissions-based notification is shown in Figure 7-12.

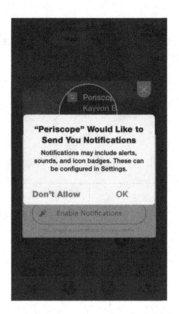

Figure 7-12. *Periscope app's standard permissions notification pop-up. This is iOS's standard notification format*

Recently however, designers have begun to rethink the way that apps are asking for permission to use their device's services. More frequently, these permissions pages are cleverly worded and designed to get a user to allow usage of a particular service that a developer feels would enhance their overall experience with the app. Shown in Figure 7-12 is an example of how video streaming app Periscope handles asking users for permission to enable notifications in the app. Note that while the standard notification will still appear, the user is primed to allow the app to use all of the necessary services from their device with a cleverly designed screen. This is undoubtedly an added step and not wholly necessary. But with users these days being overly concerned about their privacy, this additional page goes the extra mile to actually get the permissions approved where it may be instinctive to say no. Notice how in Figure 7-13 the copy entices the user to enable notifications so as not to miss out on what's going on. The bottom of the second screen in Figure 7-11 also reassures the user with the copy "Don't worry, you can choose to hide your location before each broadcast." This message is intentional and meant to show users that Periscope cares about their privacy and offers these additional controls to safeguard it for their users.

Figure 7-13. *The Periscope app does a great job of disguising the permissions process*

To enable notifications, the user hits the "Enable Notifications" button and to keep them turned off, they would hit the x in the upper right hand corner of the app. What makes this different is the wording of the request.

Creating a page just for asking for permissions gives the developer more control over the wording. The wording here is more user friendly and offers users a clearer explanation instead of what they would be missing should they turn off notifications. Here, the message reads "Enable notifications so you don't miss broadcasts from people you follow."

It is worth noting that once a user hits the Enable button the old standard notifications will still pop up and will have to be accepted. The iOS notifications would say "Periscope" would like to send you notifications. Notifications may include alerts, sounds and icon badges, etc.. That wording, by the way, is fixed and cannot be changed.

But this way, the user has a more eloquent explanation of what services the app will require before they accept or deny. If your app will require the use of more than one of the device's services, you can think about how to stagger your permissions. For example: Do you ask for permissions all at the same time? Or do you wait until a user attempts to use a feature requiring a particular service? I've seen it done both ways. This is something to think about as you are working through your app's wireframes since each page will likely require different copy and different designs.

For our PhotoBomb permission page, we'll create a simple page that asks to use the services that we will need for users to be able to experience the app to its fullest. The wireframed page is shown in Figure 7-14.

Figure 7-14. The PhotoBomb permissions page

I created the PhotoBomb permissions page by using a version of the previous new page pop-up page. Since that page already had most of the elements I needed, it was an easy choice. With a few adjustments for the size of the buttons and copy, I was able to replicate the page and make some edits to create the new permissions page. Additional embellishments will come in the design phase but this shows the structure.

Camera Capture

Increasingly, designers are changing the camera view in their apps to suit the desired experience of their apps and and to include preferences that are specific to their app for users. Certainly, you can simply use the standard iOS camera view for capture. It works just fine and offers the same basic level of functionality that every iOS user is used to. But apps that have as their main functionality image capture sometimes opt to design their own unique camera view for users. For our app, we won't be doing this but wanted to add this here as your wires should include any new or unique design elements for your camera view in this stage. You will also want to discuss this feature in particular with your developer, since this requires some special programming to be able to implement anything but the standard camera UI view. Figure 7-15 shows a few examples of special camera views that differ significantly from the standard iOS camera view, specifically, popular photo app Instagram and Evernote, the productivity app.

Figure 7-15. *Instagram and Evernote have both created unique camera capture views to align closely with the needs of their users and their brand*

I've decided that for our app, we will simplify the typical camera interface somewhat. Therefore, everything that is extraneous, or not needed for our app, we will strip away. This will leave us with what we believe to be the critical elements a user needs to take photos with our app. In Figure 7-16, we've included two specially created Delete and Approve buttons at the top of the screen and imported an image to show that the camera is live. The button in the lower center of the screen will allow the user to take a photo and the slider at the bottom is for zooming in or out on the image. Simple.

Figure 7-16. *The PhotoBomb capture screen. Users can take a picture, approve or reject, and zoom in or out*

We've just completed wireframing our PhotoBomb app's main pages using Sketch. While this process required some additional thinking in terms of how our app will work, the actual process of creating these pages was relatively simple. Figure 7-17 shows a bird's-eye view of all of our wireframes in one page in Sketch.

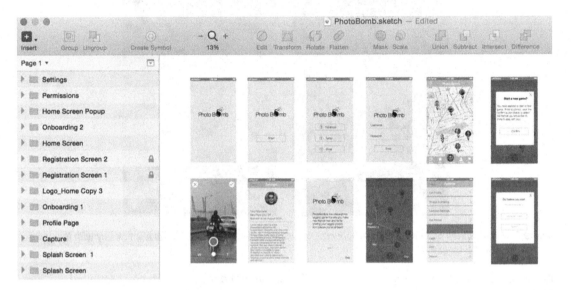

Figure 7-17. Our wireframed pages for the PhotoBomb app in Sketch

Still have doubts about working with Sketch to create your wireframes? Well, look no further. Earlier this year, former *New York Times* design director Khoi Vinh conducted a brief survey of designers called "The Tools Designers Are Using Today" to understand the most popular tools among designers today. It's a fair question to ask since as of late, there are more tools for designers to choose from when creating their designs.

Khoi asked designers their favorite tools for everything from brainstorming and wireframing, to interface design and prototyping. When the results were in from over 4000 participants in 200 countries, designers stated that their favorite tool for wireframing was Sketch, which got 27 percent of the vote and came in ahead of popular wireframing tools like Omnigraffle, Illustrator, and InDesign. A graphic from the survey website is shown in Figure 7-18. It is also important to note that Sketch was in use mostly at technology companies and startups, which have larger numbers of early adopters with freelancers and larger agencies rounding out the top numbers.

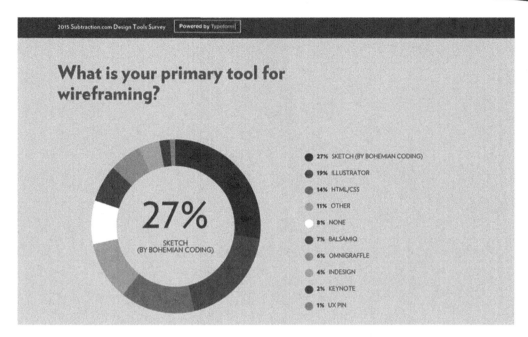

Figure 7-18. Khoi Vinh's Design Tools Survey results in Sketch as the top choice for designers in wireframing

For what it's worth, Sketch also beats all players as a designer's primary tool for interface design with 34 percent of the vote and ahead of old industry favorite Photoshop. But, we'll get into that in the next chapter.

Summary

Overall, the wireframing process is an important part of the design process. If the wireframing process is done correctly, your design process will run much smoother. While it might be tempting to rush to push pixels, take the time needed to think through your entire app in the wireframing process and make sure that the app you are designing is meeting the needs of your intended user. This can sometimes be a frustrating process, but with so many tools available on the market, whether you use one of the hi-fidelity tools listed in this chapter or good old pen and paper, this is the stage where you get to know your app and user intimately before design. This topic will be covered in the next chapter.

Chapter 8

Designing Your App

We've covered all of the basics and we've even explored using Sketch to wireframe your app. So now you're undoubtedly anxious and excited to begin actually designing your app. You will need your wireframes handy when you embark on adding color, branding, and style that come with the design phase of any app. If you're working for a client, you will have their brand guidelines and perhaps even a color palette that aligns with their brand to choose from. The elements in your wireframes may or may not carry through in your design phase, meaning that you might want to change certain icons used in your wires once you can agree on what they should be. You might even decide to create some of your icons from scratch. This will be easy to do using all of the skills that we've acquired so far. If you need to step back for a refresher, you can do that now. If not, let's jump right into designing our app.

Color

Now that we're really into the meat of the design phase, it's a good idea to talk about *color*. So far, we haven't discussed color in terms of our app, and our wireframes have excluded any real color palette or real thought about what colors will be most prominent in the PhotoBomb app.

Color can affect your app in many ways. The psychology of color has been well documented, and earlier in the book I referenced some cool online tools that can help you pick colors that work well together for the overall design of your app. If you're working on an app with clear branding guidelines, then you should refer to that document.

Most major brands have guidelines that will dictate not only what colors you can and should use in particular situations concerning that brand. They will also dictate the use of fonts, positioning, and other design elements. If you're working on an app that's primarily for your own use, branding will still be important even though you're not an established brand. For starters, it can be helpful to look at other apps in the category in which your app is positioned to see what trends are popular. However, trends come and go. With color, you want to think about how the colors you choose will affect or influence your user and, of course, overall game play. Major colors need to be offset by minor, complimentary colors that work well on the screen, especially when placed next to each other.

Also think about what colors will work well to highlight and compliment certain actions within your app. If your app is mostly photo based, then muted colors that don't compete with the photos will work best. For our PhotoBomb app, the mood should evoke familiarity and happiness. The goal is to have users feel comfortable and welcome whenever they arrive back at the home page. I like blue, and the color has been known to have calming qualities for users, so let's use blue as a starting point and use Sketch's Inspector to experiment with different hues and shades of blue as accents throughout the app.

Setting the Stage

As we begin to set up our page for design, if you haven't already set your preferences as outlined in Chapter 6, then now is a good time to do so. You should also be thinking about the size of the screen for which you will be designing. As you know, Sketch offers artboards in a variety of sizes that correspond to current iOS device screens. Before you start designing, you should decide on the target device size and select the appropriate artboard. When selecting the appropriate-size artboard, Sketch offers a selection of preset sizes, as shown in Figure 8-1.

▼ iOS Devices	
iPad Portrait	768x1024px
iPad Landscape	1024x768px
iPhone 6 Plus	414x736px
iPhone 6	375x667px
iPhone 5/5S/5C	320x568px
Apple Watch 42mm	312x390px
Apple Watch 38mm	272x340px

Figure 8-1. The list of preset artboard sizes provided in Sketch 3.3.3

Since we're designing mainly for the iPhone in this book, we will focus on these devices only. Typically, the convention is as follows:

Selecting iPhone 5, 5S, or 5C is considered designing @2×.

Designing for anything below a @2× resolution is considered @1×.

These resolutions are for the iPhone 4 series and below. Most of these devices have been discontinued, so if you're starting out, you should be designing @2× or higher. The more recent devices (iPhone 6 Plus and up) are considered @3×.

The resolution or artboard in which you start your designs will depend on the targeted devices for your final product, as well as personal preference. I typically start my designs by selecting the artboard for the iPhone 6, as it allows me to catch all of the details. Also remember that you will need to export for multiple screen sizes and resolutions when you are ready to export your assets for development.

We discuss exporting assets later in Chapter 10. For now, however, I will begin to design the screens for my app by using iPhone 6 artboards.

Splash Screen

We have our wireframes standing by and will start with our *splash screens*. Our logo is luckily already intact and we can use that directly from our wireframes. It's not a bad idea to group all of the elements in the logo and rename them for easy use. If you remember, once this is completed, we can also change the color of the logo easily and have it update across our designs for easy changes in the design phase.

As we did when we created our wireframes, we will start out with the splash screen, the first page that users will see once they've downloaded the app. Even though it will be onscreen for a short time, this page sets the stage and may even influence whether users will continue to explore your app. Therefore, it's pretty key to get this page right.

From a design perspective, the page is relatively simple. Instead of a solid color background and given the theme of the app as an app where photography is a key theme, I've decided to go with a full-screen photo background. I've checked through my folder of royalty-free images and settled on one from Death to Stockphotos. They offer a subscription-based selection of royalty-free images that are delivered to your inbox once a week. This one features a photographer with his camera. I think that image should do for now. I've imported the photo onto my Sketch canvas, resized it, added a Gaussian Blur at 10px, and repositioned our logo to be lower on the screen and to allow the user to get a better sense of the photograph. I also changed the color of the logo. The wireframe had the logo in black but I changed it to white. This allows it to stand out a bit more; remember, should we decide to change it later on, we can do so and have it update everywhere. See the key differences between the wireframe of the splash screen and the design I've just created in Figure 8-2. The wireframe is on the left with the design on the right. The important takeaways here are how the designs differ from the actual wires and how we have used and will continue to use the wireframes as a guide for the app but will feel free to deviate from them when we need to.

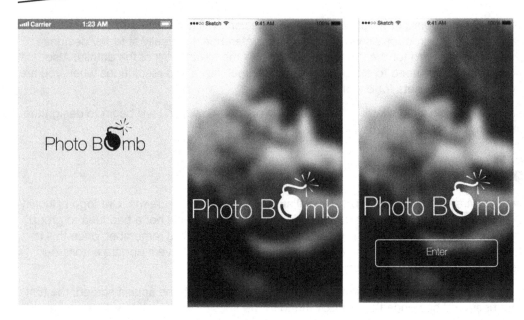

Figure 8-2. The PhotoBomb splash screens in wireframe form and in design form

The following steps were taken to create the initial screens shown in Figure 8-2.

1. Create a new blank artboard.

2. Import a desired image.

3. Add a Gaussian Blur by selecting the image and clicking the check box in the Inspector panel.

4. Adjust the Gaussian Blur settings to 10px, either by using the slider or by typing in the number in the field.

5. Duplicate the PhotoBomb logo and add it to the page.

6. Change the logo's color.

To add the Enter button:

1. Select the rectangle shape from the Insert menu.

2. Create a rounded rectangle that is 298 × 65.

3. Use the text tool from the Insert menu to add a label for the button.

4. Group these items (rectangle and label) for easy reference and to keep them together in case you need to edit them, as shown in Figure 8-3.

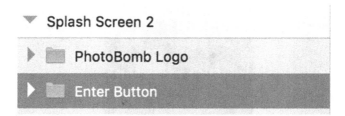

Figure 8-3. The Enter button group contains the rectangle shape as well as the button's label. The PhotoBomb logo is shown as a symbol

With our splash screens completed, we can move on to the rest of our designs. One of the great advantages of working in Sketch is not only the ease of use and low barrier to entry as we've seen throughout the book, but also how cuts down on the time it takes to complete your designs. While I am a big fan of taking the time you need to properly think through wireframes, your design phase is where you want to really save time. Design can be tedious, especially for more complex designs. Once you are up to speed with Sketch, you will undoubtedly cut down on your design time. If your design time has not been significantly reduced when using Sketch compared to Photoshop and some other design tools, then as they say, you're doing it wrong. Let's move on to the authentication screens of our PhotoBomb app.

Onboarding

Our wireframing screens for *onboarding* consisted of two screens only. But we will change things up a bit for the design phase. As mentioned, onboarding has become very important in app design in recent years. Here, we want to take some time to express some creativity and really also use our design sensibilities to entice the user and tell a story about our app.

We will duplicate our previous pages for a new screen. Once we've added them to the appropriate artboard in our design canvas, we'll then find a new image for the background of this new page. Here in the design phase and specifically in onboarding, we want to think of each screen of our app as a journey the user is taking. Where the previous page was an introduction to the app and the image showed someone with a camera, we'd love to, in some way, use the new background for this image and the series in general as a continuation of that journey we started on the previous page. Here, I've opted for a photo that would exemplify an actual image in the app. The image is of the Golden Gate Bridge in San Francisco. I'll use a few other images to take the user on that journey and add some copy to the onboarding screens where I will explain to the user what the app is all about. The copy and the imagery combined are critical to the app and to engaging first-time users. For most of them, this is the first and last time that they will see these screens. Most onboarding screens are only set to be shown on first view but can sometimes be accessible later or in the settings if a user desires to view them again. I'm focusing here on the text and images mostly. Here's what I ended up with in Figure 8-4.

Figure 8-4. A series of three onboarding screens for the PhotoBomb app. Note the combination of copy and text to tie the visuals together and take the user on a journey

The onboarding screens were created using the same techniques that we used to create the splash screens. You should now know how to import images, copy over the logo, and add text. The page controllers at the bottom of each screen are symbols copied over from the iOS template included with Sketch. Finally, to increase the legibility of the copy on each screen, I created a mask by following the these steps:

1. Create a rectangle that is the same size as your artboard.

2. Select black (FFFFF) as the fill color.

3. Move the layer into position so that it covers your artboard completely.

4. Decrease the opacity of the rectangle to 33 percent.

5. Position the layer just above the image itself in the Layers list.

This is also a good place to start thinking and talking about animations and how your elements will move on the page. Note that the PhotoBomb logo in our initial splash screens are in a different position than in our onboarding screens as we needed to adjust the size of the logo and its positioning to make room for the copy on the onboarding screen. How, then, do we transition between the two screens? This is where designer and developer must come together to discuss these transitions. They may seem easy and simple in thought, but timing is everything. A cut from the home screen to the other will likely be jarring for the user and cause a "jump-cut"-like effect with the logo jumping from one position on one screen to the other, and the text simply popping into place. A more subtle and welcoming transition here would be to have the splash screen slowly dissolve into the onboarding screen after the user hits the Enter button. Once the background has changed, the logo can shift and slide up in a way that does not surprise the user.

Another thing to note here is that we've used the Gaussian Blur effect on the first onboarding screen but have removed it from the subsequent screens. This shift can be handled as well by subtly dissolving from one image to another. In some cases, the designer must also think about how the user is interacting with the screens to move through the app. That is to say, is the user swiping or tapping on the screen to advance the onboarding flow? Most users will swipe or tap as these are natural touch interface interactions. In some instances, the page will bump slightly prompting the user to swipe to see the next screen. These are interaction and transition details that, again, can be handled either with annotations, with the creation of a simple prototype, or with a conversation with your developer.

Authentication

Our designed *authentication* pages will hold fairly true to the wireframed pages. If a user has gotten this far in the app, they are primed and ready to register, or so we hope. The point of these pages is to show branded buttons for Facebook and Twitter so that a user can choose their favorite social networks quickly, getting into the app and on to game play as soon as possible. We will brand the buttons to match the appropriate shades of blue for both Twitter and Facebook as well. It makes their brands easily recognizable.

We'll create our page by duplicating one of our previous pages and deleting the background images. After we find an appropriate image for this page, we'll optimize, import, and resize it to fit our screen and ensure that it doesn't make our overall file size too big as photographs tend to do.

I want to keep the sizes of our buttons consistent across the app, so I'll copy the button from the splash screen onto our page and duplicate it three times to create the three authentication buttons that we need. Once we have them in place, we need to adjust the colors (the duplicated buttons were clear), rename the labels, and add the appropriate icons.

Since the authentication screens represent a new flow for the user, we will create a new page as well to differentiate this flow from the onboarding/splash screen flow. This will make it easier for us to present and show the work if necessary. When designing, it's important to remember that presentation and organization are important in your work.

We can easily distribute the space between the buttons by checking to see how far they are apart from each other, making sure they're centered vertically and horizontally on the screen using our guidelines, and then move on to styling each button accordingly. We'll handle the Facebook button first. This button will be, as in the wireframe, branded with a Facebook "F" logo and will be Facebook's unique shade of blue. In my opinion, spelling out the name is unnecessary, as almost everyone on the planet by now is aware of the social network. To get the appropriate shade of Facebook blue, I'll simply open up a new browser page to Facebook, select the color from the Inspector, and use the dropper tool to "steal" the color from the page. This is one of Sketch's handiest features. It makes color matching in designing and wireframes so easy. With our Facebook button completed, we'll move on and do the same for the Twitter button. As of this moment, I was thinking that the e-mail button will stay clear so that we can still see the background image behind it. However, after trying this approach, I've decided to make the e-mail button a solid color to match the others above.

I've imported by icons for the buttons via Pixel Love, resized and colored them to match, and set a style for the button labels so that they, as well, are consistent. Once the icons have been added we can zoom out on our canvas and have a look at our newly created authentication page. You can see what it looks like in Figure 8-5.

Figure 8-5. Our branded and designed authentication page for the PhotoBomb app

Bear in mind that the idea with these pages is to create a seamless transition between each page. The PhotoBomb logo should be in the same position on each page and the elements on each page should subtly shift as the user transitions to a new page. Should a user decide to go back in the process or to the previous page, the elements should shift in reverse. My goal, is to afford the user ultimate control over the entire process in every flow. Remember that our ultimate goal here is to entice the user with a very clear idea of what to expect once they do register and begin to use our app. This experience is preparation for the overall in-app experience and what the user sees now will set the stage for what they experience in the app.

E-mail Registration

Our authentication flow is complete for our app. We can now move on to the *e-mail registration* page. This consists of our logo, fields for a user to enter their username and password, and an Enter button. Pretty straightforward, right? Our username and password labels will be the same size as the previous page's labels. There's that consistency thing again. And instead of actually drawing a line (which Sketch allows and easily accommodates), we will create a 1-pixel rectangle that we will use for each field and duplicate it to create both fields.

This page is can actually be considered to be a part of the authentication flow. Here, however, we will add a few things that are not included in our wireframes. For example: typically when passwords are typed, they are obscured somehow. Here, the in the design phase, we get to select how the password is protected and what creative technique we will use to mask the user's password. Masking passwords is a common practice, but the approach can differ from app to app. There is also a school of thought that says that password masking on sign up or registration is bad user experience (UX) because users end up making more mistakes, especially when they are required to type a password twice. If a user is asked to type their password twice and both passwords need to match to register, then it makes sense that masking both passwords can be tricky for users who have more complicated passwords. So, some designers opt to only mask passwords on sign in when a user has already chosen their passwords and in theory know it well.

While this is a very real issue, we're going to forego that for now and assume that this issue doesn't exist. This is likely an issue that should have been assessed and decided in the wireframing stage of the project. Thinking about how we will creatively mask the password is another issue so we'll focus on that and assume that the decision has been made and we are all in agreement.

The typical way to mask passwords is by using an asterisk or by using circles. I masked the password using circles in Figure 8-6. Keeping them empty gives it a nice touch and brings through the background image which again is critical at this stage in the app.

Figure 8-6. For the password and user authentication pages, I used empty circles as password masks and the same style applied in the PhotoBomb app

Home Page

Our *home page*, as we know, is the most important page in our app. As we've established in our wireframes, our home page is the page that users arrive at when they register and return to after completing any tasks on other pages in the app. Therefore, to complete the journey that we started when the user initially became familiar with the app, this page must, in some way, be familiar to the user. But how can a page that a user has never seen before be familiar? Here, it helps to step back and review all of our designed pages from a bird's-eye view to fully familiarize ourselves with the flow so far.

I do this often to make sure that I can continue the overall flow of the app and begin to think conceptually about how I want the app to continue from a creative standpoint.

The home page as wireframed was lacking some critical elements and now that we're designing it, we will need to add and refine them. Starting with the tab bar, where I used the icons used in the wireframe templating kit, I've decided to select more appropriate icons that align more closely with the actions that they represent and added a highlight bar that is intended to highlight the user's current page with a small thin bar under the tab icon's title that moves along the bottom of the screen. I selected the icons that I thought would be familiar to users to represent the associated actions. These are personal design choices that I made here—you may agree or disagree with them—so feel free to explore how or why you would take a different approach to your design.

While I'm still using the map background as the main home screen and overall game play, I had to make some specific changes to the way that the player's friends appeared on the screen. While the wires used blue map icons to show the position of friends and a red icon to denote the location of the player on the home screen, I began to feel as though both elements took up too much space on the game's screen. So, I decided to combine them. It would present a cleaner interface and the screen would remain clutter free.

To do this, I created a new Sketch file and imported both visuals onto the screen. After bringing them closer and pushing the map icon behind the profile image. This helped me to visualize how I wanted the new icon to look. I then created a new shape that replicated the map pin and shadow. I grouped all of the shapes together and created a symbol so I could change colors if I need to at a later date across all icons on the screen. The final results are shown in Figure 8-7. While some of the individual images could use some slight adjustments, you can see the general idea.

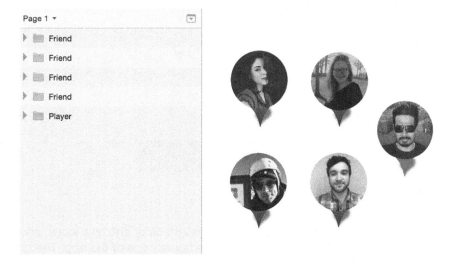

Figure 8-7. Recreating the new markers for the player and friends for the PhotoBomb home page

With the icons completed, I was able to import them back into the newly designed home page shown in Figure 8-8.

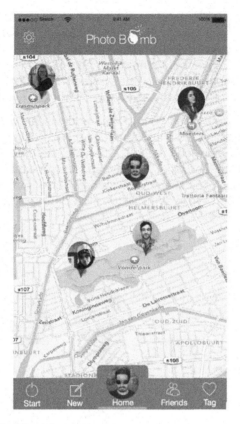

Figure 8-8. Final design of the PhotoBomb home page

The new page includes our main color of blue, our highlight color, the final icons, and the layout of what the user will see when they arrive at the home page of the app. The tab bar was brought over from the wireframes and re-edited for the design phase. I changed the color and also adjusted the size of the tab bar to accommodate the new icons, title, and the highlight bar.

With this page complete, we can move on to our other pages from the wireframes that round out the rest of the PhotoBomb app.

As an aside and in keeping with utilizing the skills we have learned so far in the book about how to create and organize a sketch file, I am remembering to appropriately name my layers, groups, and symbols as I move through the design. It makes it easier to find things when they need to be adjusted and will also help greatly when we are ready to export our designs and hand them over to a developer. I now have multiple pages in my Sketch document and every layer is named and titled for easy reference. Every phase of the app has been placed on a separate page to keep things clean. This also makes it easier if for some reason, a new page has to be added. You can see the Layers list so far in Figure 8-9. If you're moving too fast in your designs, take some time to go back and group and title layer appropriately. It will take a few minutes to clean things up but it will save lots of time if you need to hand off your files to someone else.

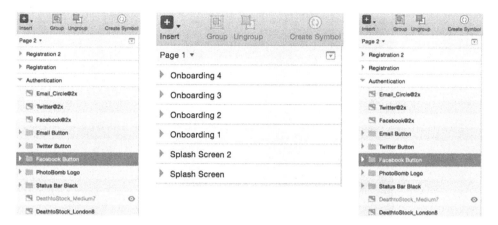

Figure 8-9. Layers list of the PhotoBomb app with titles and pages

Settings

Up next to be designed is our *Settings* page. This page is where users will come to manage elements of their app such as privacy, the aforementioned radius of game play in their games, and privacy information like who can see them in the app. The design for this page will be relatively simple. We will use a standard table view as shown in the wireframes from the first level of the settings page.

Pages with a table view are standard in iOS and should probably be one of the first pages that any designer for iOS learns to design. The table view is a common design pattern in iOS because it is a great way to display information in a hierarchy, and as such this is usually included in some of the more popular iOS design templates, including the one that is pre-packaged with Sketch. To grab the table view symbol that you can use, go to the File menu and select New from template. The iOS Design option should be listed, and you can select it from there. Once the template opens, you can copy the table view symbol over to your current project and customize it to suit your design.

Our Settings page will be created by creating a new screen in portrait with status bar and background and we'll import table view symbols from the iOS template. Once this is done, we must customize them to match our app's color scheme. Using the eyedropper, we can update the table view symbols and change the labels on each one, and then our page has been created as shown in Figure 8-10.

Figure 8-10. Settings page with table views designed

Profile Page

As I look back on the *profile page* as presented in the wireframes, I see that it could use some improvements. Currently as shown in the wires, there's simple information on the user as well as a field for city and state. But, I'm thinking of taking a different approach to this page than what is shown in the wireframes. Undoubtedly, this situation could arise when you are working in the real world. There will be times when you want to make a change in the design phase. If you're the person responsible for the wires, this shouldn't be a big problem. But if not, it's always a good idea to get consensus. Honestly, it's a good idea to get consensus anyway. But we'll assume here that the decision is being driven by another force, perhaps a client, an account person, or even a creative director. This means it has to happen, and sooner rather than later. How do you make changes in the design phase that could potentially affect the user flow of your app? Luckily, the changes we will make won't do that, but it's worth exploring this. If time allows, you can go back to your wires and quickly mock up the page and revise the flow there. Also very important to get everyone on the team's buy-in to be able move quickly.

Also, examine the flow a few steps forward and a few steps back. This is to make sure that you aren't doing anything that will affect your overall flow and user experience. When I look at the changes that I would like to make in my profile page, I've already assessed that this won't really affect very much. I am just going to expand the content on the page a bit. Easy, right? We'll see. Let's discuss the changes I'd like to make. When viewing your profile page, you want to find out more about the user as it relates to game play. A profile page isn't only viewable to the user; it will also be available to view by other players or friends in the game. What information would they find important? Those are some of the questions that I asked myself when considering my redesign for the profile. The results of my redesign are shown in Figure 8-11.

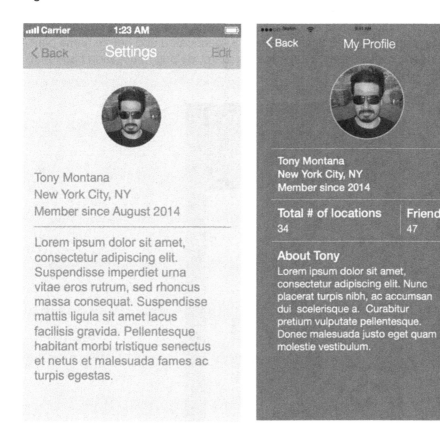

Figure 8-11. Newly designed profile page with new content and Edit button. Next to it is the original wireframe

What changed in the page is subtle but makes, I think, for a better-looking profile page. We've added two sections that show the total number of locations that the user is associated with as well as the number of friends he has and then followed up with the biographical information which can be placed in the "About" section at the bottom of the page. I also added a light blue border around the profile image. Remember, light blue is our highlight color from the home page of the app. It's a nice touch to maintain branding consistency through the app.

Permissions

I've talked about how *permissions* are enjoying a new and improved look in iOS apps these days. So, I wanted to try something different here. Since PhotoBomb will need access to the user's camera and location, I added these options to let users know up front what we will need from them. There are many ways to do this but the most successful ways are via effective design and copy. I don't claim to be a copywriter so perhaps the copy on the permissions in Figure 8-12 could use some polish, but the page, from a design standpoint, does its job. The pop-up appears after a user has been authenticated and before game play. Once a user hits the Confirm button, they will get the standard, default notification page that iOS provides.

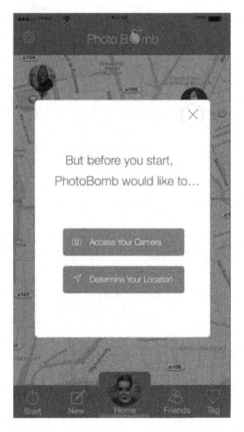

Figure 8-12. Permissions page with pop-up and dimmed home screen in the background

The page was created by grabbing and duplicating the home page as is, and creating a black rectangle to cover the screen and then decreasing its opacity to allow the home page to show through. The idea here is that the home page will be dimmed while the pop-up is onscreen. Once the user closes the window or confirms, the pop-up disappears and the background brightens back to its normal state. The pop-up window is a rectangle with a border radius of 11. Buttons are the same size as all of the other buttons used so far in the app with icons from Pixel Love. One note on the icons is that I wanted to use a camera icon and a location icon that users would be familiar with from their interaction with iOS, as these are pretty close. The Close button was created by hand; I created a cross with two rectangles with the same length and a width of 3 pixels. I created a cross and then rotated it to create the "X" and then added it to a circle shape. These three shapes are then combined into a symbol so that it can be easily reused.

Camera Capture

Our last designed screen will be the capture screen. From the wireframes you will remember that we decided to create our own *camera capture* screen to align closer with the goals of the app. This is not necessary but a nice touch. Note that the "X" and check mark icons are red and green, respectively, and the Take Picture button is our branded shade of PhotoBomb blue (see Figure 8-13).

Figure 8-13. *PhotoBomb camera capture screen*

This final page brings us to the end of our design phase for our app. I've attempted to choose pages that are critical to the overall functionality of the app and also that allows you to use the best features of Sketch to make your design phase and workflow as seamless as possible. You should now have a great set of designs that you can be comfortable with.

In the next chapter, we'll discuss designing your app's icon, which has become an increasingly important facet of the design phase and one that can benefit from the use of Sketch.

Summary

We've covered designing multiple pages of the PhotoBomb app in this chapter. Most of the techniques that we've covered should already be familiar to you. We designed our onboarding screens and some of the other main screens that make up the PhotoBomb application. You should review and familiarize yourself with the steps outlined in each section for each page so that you can recreate them. Surely, while these pages represent some popular effects and mobile design patterns, it is equally important for you to develop your own sense of design. So, while it's great to replicate the steps, be sure to experiment with different effects and styles of your own.

Developing your own style and visual language is an important part of becoming a designer. Once you are happy with your designs, you can move on to designing your app's icon, which is what we will cover in the next chapter.

Chapter 9

Designing Your App's Icon

So far, we've wireframed our app and designed it. You might be thinking that we're just about ready to hand off the designs to be built, and in some cases, depending on your process and workflow, this may be true. But if you're like me, you will want to continue the design process and work on your app's icon as well. Previously considered an afterthought, app icon design is now pretty much its very own art form. For example, there are designers who focus solely on designing App icons as a specialty. If you do a search for app icons you'll find lots of articles and discussions, some how-to's, and even some app icon generators. A word to the wise: if your app's icon is important to you, stay away from turnkey app icon generators.

Your app's icon is the first thing that users will likely see as they peruse the App Store. So, you want it to be unique and well designed. These days, there's no excuse for a badly designed app icon. And quite honestly, having a badly designed icon can make the difference between a hit app with hundreds or even thousands of downloads and none at all. When I look through the App Store to check out new apps, before I read a description of what an app is or does, I look at the icon. If it's not up to snuff, I keep it moving. I dare say that most consumers are like me. With over a million apps in the Apple App Store alone, consumers don't have much time to read app descriptions and reviews. Usually, an app's icon will make all the difference to them. So, it's an important part of the design process and your branding and marketing for your app.

This chapter is dedicated to app icons. We'll discuss why an app's icon is so important, what makes a great app icon, and then go through the process of designing an icon for our PhotoBomb app.

First, it's a good idea to read the Human Interface Guidelines first to see what Apple has to say about designing your icon. This should be your de facto go-to list for creating your icon. Every app needs an icon and your app will not be accepted into the App Store without it. So, it behooves you to think very earnestly about what your icon will convey about your app. The icon will be used across iOS to represent your app, so it will need to be reproduced in many different sizes.

From the Apple's Human Interface Guidelines, here's a list of do's and don'ts:

1. Use universal imagery that people will recognize.

2. Embrace simplicity.

3. Create an abstract interpretation of your app's main idea.

4. Avoid transparency.

5. Don't use replicas of iOS interface elements or Apple's hardware products.

Since icons are in use all over iOS, the Human Interface Guidelines also outline exactly what sizes these icons are meant to be. Since all apps must have an icon, there's a handy table included for designers to reference that outlines sizes requires for all icons and images.

I've included a selection from the Human Interface Guidelines in Figure 9-1.

Asset	iPhone 6s Plus and iPhone 6 Plus (@3x)	iPhone 6s, iPhone 6, and iPhone 5 (@2x)	iPhone 4s (@2x)	iPad and iPad mini (@2x)	iPad 2 and iPad mini (@1x)	iPad Pro (@2x)
App icon (required for all apps)	180 x 180	120 x 120	120 x 120	152 x 152	76 x 76	167 x 167
App icon for the App Store (required for all apps)	1024 x 1024	1024 x 1024	1024 x 1024	1024 x 1024	1024 x 1024	1024 x 1024
Launch file or image (required for all apps)	Use a launch file (see Launch Files)	For iPhone 6s and iPhone 6, use a launch file (see Launch Files) For iPhone 5, 640 x 1136	640 x 960	1536 x 2048 (portrait) 2048 x 1536 (landscape)	768 x 1024 (portrait) 1024 x 768 (landscape)	2048 x 2732 (portrait) 2732 x 2048 (landscape)

Figure 9-1. *Table from Apple's Human Interface Guidelines showing requirements for icon sizes*

What Makes a Great App?

With the sheer number of apps in the App Store, how do you create an app that grabs folks' attention as they scroll and swipe by? Well, in addition to the points made by the Human Interface Guidelines, there are a few basic tenets of app icon design that you'll want to bear in mind as you design your app. Let's explore them.

Avoid Words

App icons are small. When a user is viewing the app charts, the size of app icons they see along with the app's name are **57 × 57**. That's not very big. So, what can your app say without actually saying anything? Plenty. This is not to say that some app icons don't have words on them. This isn't a hard–and-fast rule. A scroll through the App Store will reveal that there are still plenty of app icons that have words on them. However, you will also note that many others don't. Most of the apps with words on their icons appear to be games and whimsical apps. Also, consider this. Words are easy. Without words, you must really engage in a design exercise to think about how to convey the central idea of your app without telling users what to expect. Much like we discussed the overall storytelling involved in designing your app when we explored the onboarding pages, so too, we must think about how the icon engages the user visually and conveys the idea of the app to user before they've even downloaded it.

Figure 9-2 shows some screenshots from the App Store. As you can see, this selection shows some of the top features and top-grossing apps in the Apple App Store at the time of this writing. Most of them use no words on their icons.

Figure 9-2. Top charts from the Apple App Store show that most popular apps use no words on icons

Use Colors Wisely

The next thing you'll want to remember when considering a design for your app icons is to be very careful with the colors you choose. If you have branding that includes a color palette already for your app, then you want to stick to that to be consistent. Even so, you won't need to include all of the colors in the palette on your icon. Ask yourself what color represents your brand best and would also make your app stand out the most in the App Store. If you have a color that is already quite prominently used throughout your app, consider that or a shade of that color for use as the background for your icon.

Contrast is great, too. If your icon features a specific or unique shape, you will want to it to stand out against your background color. For sure, a white shape against a colored background is one of the more popular combinations for App Store icons that I've seen. But you can go another route if you can make it work. A few of my favorite app icons are shown in Figure 9-3. Among them are examples of some of the most popular brands we know and others which may not be as popular. Craftsy, for example, chose to add their name to their icon but note how it stands out from the background and is easy to read. Also, Green Kitchen does a great job of creating an icon that uses what appears to be a photograph or realistic design to let browsers know exactly what the brand is about.

Figure 9-3. Popular app icons from the Apple App Store

Keep It Simple

Icons are small, yes. 57×57 isn't a lot of space. But, it is still possible to create something that conveys your app's main idea within that very limited space. The best way to do this is to keep your idea simple. The apps shown in Figure 9-3 do the very most with the little space afforded to create an icon, and they do it very well. Think about how you want user to think about your app in the simplest of terms and then start to design around that. This will require lots of editing. You might start with an entire word and trim it down to one letter. Or you might start with a word and create an image that evokes the felling of that word better than the word could. Brainstorming is helpful here and then multiple iterations to bring the idea down to a single visual that users will see and be able to associate with your app immediately. But take it from me and some of the best-designed apps in the App Store: simplicity is key.

Be Inspired by Others

Stealing is wrong, but when it comes to design, it's totally ok to use other designers' work as inspiration for your own. For some, this may be a slippery slope and, to be clear, I would never advocate stealing someone else's work. But if you're new to icon design and haven't yet developed a knack for it, then you should definitely spend some time on the App Store perusing some of the more popular apps, their design, and yes, their icons. Support these designers by downloading their apps and exploring their design style and aesthetic. While doing this you just might find some inspiration for your own app and icon. Now, let's move onto actually designing our PhotoBomb app icon.

Designing Your Icon with Sketch

As Sketch is an Apple-centric product, as with other templates, the program comes with a template for designing your iOS icon as well. These days, it also offers a template for those designing for Android. But we are here to talk about iOS design. As such, we will further explore the template for designing your iOS app's icon and subsequently use it to design our own.

As with everything else that we've done so far with our fictional app, I started with a pencil-and-paper sketch to get the general idea out of my head. Sometimes, I have more than one idea and will create high-level sketches of each one. Sometimes, I'll combine more than one idea into a composite. Figure 9-4 is a photo of a pencil-based sketch of my proposed icon for the PhotoBomb app. While it may seem rudimentary, it is enough for me to grasp the basic concepts that I'd like to include in the app's icon design.

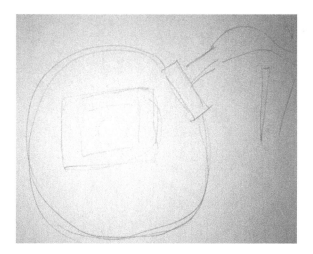

Figure 9-4. *Initial sketch for the PhotoBomb app icon*

As shown previously, the sketch shows a bomb with an image of a camera in side of it. The bomb is reminiscent of the bomb used in the PhotoBomb logo we used on the inside pages of the app although there are key differences in the way they appear. I wanted the bomb on the icon to be slightly different. So, how did I create the icon from this basic sketch?

First, I started with Sketch's iOS icon template. As you can see in Figure 9-5, the template includes all of the anticipated icon sizes once you open the template. There are templates for the App Store, Spotlight search, and settings. For our app design, we won't use all of the other templates, so I deleted the others so that I could focus on the main icon. Figure 9-5 shows all of the templates on first launch of the App icon template.

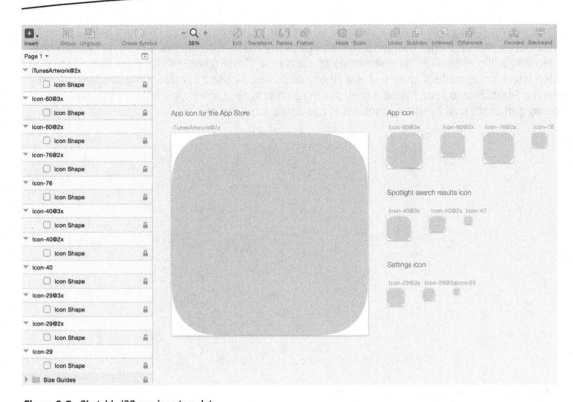

Figure 9-5. *Sketch's iOS app icon template*

Set the Background Color

Once I deleted all of the other icon layers I changed the color of the background of the icon. I considered the lighter shade of blue we used in the app for the highlight color but in an effort to present a bolder icon with more contrast, decided to go with the darker blue used throughout the app (Hex code 4A90E2). That way, whatever we do on top should stand out a bit more. One thing to note is that when we create an icon for inclusion in iOS, we will be submitting the icon as a perfect square. The rounded corners are added later by iOS. The template includes the rounded corners as a layer, so I will turn that layer off and focus on the entire artboard. From time to time, I will turn the layer on to get a sense of what our final icon will look like, and this toggling back and forth is represented in the images to follow.

Creating the Bomb Icon

Next, I set about using shapes to create the bomb icon. Here are the steps I took to create it.

1. Select the Oval shape from the Insert menu.

2. Holding down the Shift key, and draw a perfect 700 × 700 circle.

3. Remove the border for now and select black as the fill color.

4. Create a rectangle of 170 × 272 by selecting it from the Insert menu.

5. Give the rectangle a border radius of 11.

6. Move the rectangle to the upper right corner of the circle and rotate it into position.

7. Create another rectangle of 322 × 158.

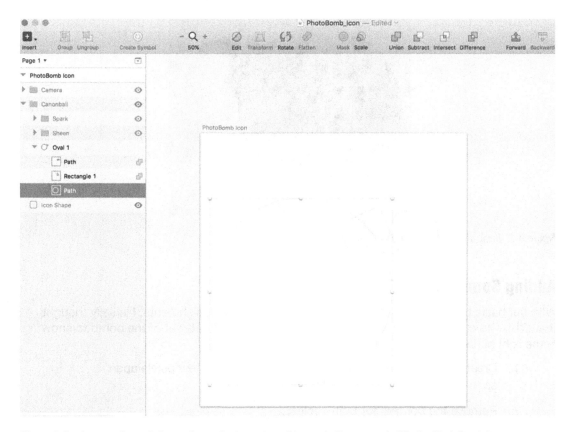

Figure 9-6. shows paths and shapes for each element used to create the cannonball in the PhotoBomb icon

To create the fuse:

1. Rotate the new rectangle into place so that it appears to be protruding from the other rectangle.

2. Double-click the rectangle to bring up Sketch's Bezier curve options.

3. Using a combination of the straight and mirrored options, adjust the rectangle to add some curvature to the straight lines in the rectangle.

4. Select all three shapes and combine them using the Union button from the Boolean Operations menu.

With the steps outlined above, my icon design is shown in Figure 9-7.

Figure 9-7. Basic shapes combined to create our bomb

Adding Some Shine

With our basic bomb shape created, we can move onto embellishments. I initially thought that I'd like to create some shine or sheen on the lower left quadrant of the bomb to show some light hitting it. To do this, I took the following steps:

1. Create two identical white circles and move them a few pixels apart so that you are able to see both.

2. Remove the borders for both circles.

3. Select both and use the Subtract button from the Boolean Operations menu.

4. Change one of the resulting shapes to a light gray color and reduce the opacity to 34 percent. I used Hex code 9B9B9B.

The results of these actions are shown in Figure 9-8.

Figure 9-8. *I've added some light hitting the bomb from the bottom*

Creating the Spark

Every fuse has a spark, right? So let's create one for our bomb. It really doesn't get easier than this with Sketch. Here are the steps to creating the spark for our bomb.

1. Select the star shape from the Insert menu and draw a start onto your canvas at the end of the fuse of the bomb.

2. Go to the Inspector and increase the number of points on the start to 12.

3. Remove the border and change the fill color to Hex code F5A623.

4. Repeat steps 1 and 2 to create a new star.

5. Move the new star a few pixels away from the first star.

6. Remove the border of the second star and change the fill color to F8E71C.

You should now have a spark at the end of the fuse and your icon design should look like the graphic in Figure 9-9.

Figure 9-9. The PhotoBomb app icon with the newly added spark at the end of the fuse

Now that our spark has been added, our icon is really starting to take shape. Going back to our initial advice on designing app icons, I want users to be able to look at the app and get a very clear idea of what the app is about and what they can do. The word PhotoBomb typically means that a photo has been bombed or spoiled by another person entering into the frame and ruining the shot. Our app is not about that. So, how do we give potential users a very clear sense of what this app is about? Well, that's where the camera comes into play. But, will it really fit inside the bomb? Well, it required removing the shine that we just added. But, this is a necessary part of the design process.

Let's begin. First, let's group and hide the sheen layers so they are out of the way.

1. Select all that make up the sheen on the bomb image.

2. Select the Group button in the Header menu to create a new folder containing the shapes.

3. Rename the group "Sheen" or some variation of the word so you can easily find this group.

4. Hover over the menu and click the eye icon that appears to hide them from the canvas.

The results are shown in Figure 9-10.

Figure 9-10. We now have cleaned up and titled layers appropriately and hidden the sheen so that we can continue with business of adding the camera to the icon

Adding the Camera!

Next, let's add the camera. Sure, we could import an icon of a camera but, here, we want to put to good use all of the skills we've developed in the previous chapters. With Sketch, we can create our very own camera icon using shapes we can easily create. Here are the steps to create the camera:

First, we will create the camera body.

1. Create a 412 × 290 rectangle with a corner radius of 46.

2. Remove the fill and give the border a thickness of 12.

Next, we'll create the lens.

1. Select the oval tool from the Insert menu:

2. Hold the Shift key while drawing the circle to make it perfect circle of 214 × 214.

3. Go to the Inspector tool to give the circle a thickness of 12.

4. Use ↑ + D to make a duplicate of the first circle.

5. Resize the second circle to 162 × 162 and give this new circle a thickness of 7.

6. Position the second circle inside the first.

We'll create the flash on top of the camera next:

1. Create another rectangle by selecting the rectangle tool from the Insert menu.

2. Go to the Inspector tool and give it a thickness of 12.

3. Double-click the shape to bring up the Bezier tools.

4. Select the Straight tool and drag the two top corners closer together to create the shape of the flash.

5. Move this new shape to the top of the camera body shape.

To create the Take Picture button:

1. Select the oval from the Insert menu.

2. Hold the Shift key while drawing the circle to make it a perfect circle of 32 × 32.

3. Go to the Inspector tool to give the circle a thickness of 7.

4. Position the circle in the upper right corner of the camera body.

Our camera has now been created. I've hidden the other layers of the icon including the bomb, fuse, and spark so that I could focus on the camera. Figure 9-11 shows the camera we've just created on the canvas without the other elements.

Figure 9-11. The completed camera icon that will be added to the rest of the design

With the camera icon completed, we are now ready to put everything together to see how our final app icon will look.

To make my final adjustments, I'll need to unhide all of the other layers on the canvas to ensure that they all work well. To do this, I'll just click the eye on every layer that has been hidden and watch them reappear on the canvas. After making my final adjustments in spacing, the final icon can be seen in Figure 9-12. It may not be the best icon in the world, but it holds fast to some of our principles outlined earlier in the chapter. If you have time, you may want to put the app before an informal focus group to see if potential users can glean what the app is about.

Figure 9-12. *The completed PhotoBomb app icon*

Other Changes for Consistency

Now that the PhotoBomb icon is complete, I decided to go back and change the old logo we'd been using on the onboarding pages and in the header of the main app. To do this, I needed to create a smaller version of the bomb icon only, one that would fit in between the letters of our logo. To do this I made a duplicate of the icon and deleted the camera, as it would be too small to show. Then I resized the bomb icon and changed the fill color from black to white and added it to the logo. I grouped the layers and created a new logo symbol so that any additional changes or adjustments would be reflected across my designs. The new onboarding screens with the new bomb icon in the log are shown in Figure 9-13.

Figure 9-13. Onboarding screens with redesigned bomb icon in the logo

Our app icon is complete. The process of going back and making final adjustments happens in most stages of the design process. Most projects won't easily flow from one phase to the other. There may be lots of backtracking and making changes midstream. The key to being a good designer is to always remain flexible at any stage in the process. Each shift or change will bring a fair amount of learning with it.

We've wrapped up our designs, created an app icon we're pretty happy with, and made our final adjustments. We're now ready to hand off our designs to an engineer for development. The next chapter will take us through that process.

Chapter 10

Exporting Your Assets for Development

Your app is designed, and everything has been approved. Your clients are happy and you're celebrating another win with your creative team for a job well done. But not so fast! Now that your app is all designed and about to be made into a real live application available for download, you'll need to hand off those designs to your engineer or development team. And while how an app looks is of great importance, it is also important that it works well. This requires some collaboration between the designer and developer.

As the line between design and development blurs, points of integration between design and development have become a necessary part of the app development life cycle. Designers are becoming more comfortable with code and developers are becoming more comfortable with design, and Sketch is a big part of that. These days, it is not uncommon to see Sketch design classes bundled with Swift development classes so that designers can complement their design skills with some development as well. And with Sketch, it has never been easier to export your assets for use in Xcode.

If you're not developing your app yourself and you have a developer to do the work, you'll want to have a conversation to understand just how your developer would prefer to have assets handed off. This is true especially if you haven't been taking a collaborative approach to your design and including your developing along the way.

In this chapter, we'll discuss the exporting functionality in Sketch 3 and how to use it, and we'll walk through how to perform specific exporting tasks for iOS. Luckily, Sketch can help here, too. Exporting assets is a common task for designers, and as a feature, this is one of Sketch's best. The program offers export options to a number of different file formats and relatively easy-to-perform exporting operations. We'll start with the basics and walk through the different ways you can use Sketch to export your assets for iOS development.

Because there are so many different resolutions to export for with iOS, you will need to be able to export for @2× and even @3×, and Sketch makes all of these possible and incredibly seamless. At the end of this chapter, you'll be ready to export your designs using Sketch for handoff.

As we have in previous chapters, we will continue to use our PhotoBomb application for all exercises in this chapter. That way, we can complete the entire design process using one set of designs and eventually export to a complete set of assets for the app.

What to Export and What Not to Export

So how do we decide what to export for our developer? Well, this is where the conversation comes in. Talking to your developer about his preferences is always a good approach. But typically, you will be exporting assets that cannot be re-created programmatically. When an app is created in Xcode, the developer rebuilds your design with code. Items such as fonts and text layers can easily be recreated in code but certain graphical elements will need to be provided to developers. Elements that could possibly change in appearance should also be exported. For example, if any item on a toolbar must illuminate or light up, on tap, then it should be exported separately. Alternately, you may want to create an "on" and an "off" version of that element and export them both for your developer so that there is a graphical representation of both states. Also, icons that are not a standard part of the iOS UI should be exported. When in doubt, export the element anyway. If your developer doesn't need it, he or she will skip it.

When exporting in Sketch you have two ways to export elements on your canvas. One way is to select Export from the Insert menu in the toolbar. The other is to click the Make Exportable button in the lower right corner of your Sketch Canvas Inspector window while a layer is selected. When the Make Exportable button is clicked as shown in Figure 10-1, Sketch will create a preview of the exported layer in the area above the button. If more than one layer is selected, all thumbnails will appear there.

Figure 10-1. The Make Exportable button before and after selecting a layer for export. In this case, we have selected the Enter button on an onboarding screen of the PhotoBomb app

When focusing on the process of exporting, there are a few areas of the canvas that you will need to keep in mind. Figure 10-2 shows the three areas of your canvas to pay attention to when exporting. From left to right in the following image, they are the Export options from the file menu (if you choose to go this route); the second is the Export option on the lower right corner of the Inspector and the slice and layer options at the bottom of the layer list.

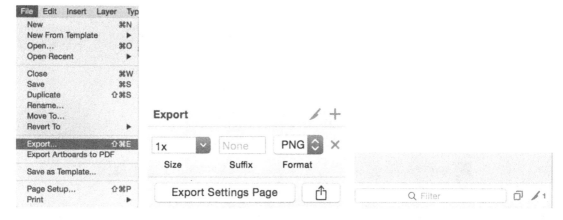

Figure 10-2. Three areas to consider when exporting assets from the Sketch canvas

The Knife

When selecting a layer for export, you will notice that the icon of the knife at the bottom of the layer list will be highlighted. The knife simply means that there are layers available for export. Any layer that has a knife next to it will show up next time you select Export from the menu in the toolbar. A drop-down will show all layers included in that export as shown in Figure 10-3; the figure shows the drop-down and selected layers for export.

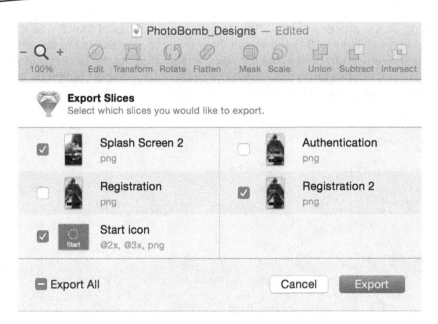

Figure 10-3. Drop-down showing slices available for export when selecting Export from the menu in the toolbar

If you go back to your layer list, you will see that all of the layers shown in Figure 10-3 will have the knife icon next to them. You can move these layers into the corresponding groups for better organization.

Slicing from the Insert Menu

To select an area for slicing or export, you can also select the Slice option from the Insert menu. Once you've done this, your cursor will turn into a small knife and you will be able to select any area in the design on your canvas for export. Once the area is selected, a preview of the slice will appear in the inspector and the knife icon below the number list will update to show the total number of slices currently on your canvas.

File Formats for Exporting

When exporting your files in Sketch, the program provides multiple options for output. They are JPEGS, PNG, TIFF, PDF, EPS, and SVG. Let's talk a little bit about these file formats.

PNG

PNG is an uncompressed graphic format that is the preferred format for exporting files for iOS. It is pretty much a what-you-see-is-what-you-get format. Nothing is really added or subtracted from the image during the exporting process. Another great thing about PNGs is that they support transparency, which means that this format won't reveal a transparent background if one is included in your graphic. PNG is the preferred file size format for Apple's IDE, Xcode, since it optimizes PNGs as part of the build process.

JPEG

JPEG is a compressed file format. This means that your final graphic file and any colors, effects, or gradients will be compressed and will have fewer colors than existed in our original file. The JPEG file will also be considerably smaller than a PNG when exported. If you're exporting an artboard just to show someone the progress of your work where compression and colors won't matter, JPEG is a good choice.

TIFF

TIFF is another uncompressed graphic file format; it is considered a standard for delivering printed images like photographs. You will likely rarely ever deliver a TIFF file to someone working on interface design for the Web or mobile.

All of the three image formats shown previously are considered raster images.

> **Tip**   Photoshop (PSDs) and Illustrator (AI) files are not supported for export by Sketch.

The following file formats support vector graphics and are good options if you have to send to those who will be editing the image.

PDF

This file format is a popular format used across the Web. PDFs retain the vector nature of vector objects and text in the file and can be scaled up or down.

EPS

This file format is best if you are sending this to someone who will be editing the file from an Adobe program like Illustrator. EPS stands for Encapsulated Post Script, but these days, most Adobe programs have their own proprietary file formats.

SVG

Typically, icons and logos and other two-dimensional graphics are created and exported as SVG. SVG stands for Scalable Vector Graphics and typically supports some level of animation or interactivity.

Size Options for Exporting

Sketch provides multiple options for exporting your work in different sizes. Clicking on the size drop-down in the Inspector will reveal a number of preset sizes in which Sketch can export your artboards and images. You can use a multiplier such as any number followed by x to increase the exported image by that number. Presets are 0.5×, 1×, 2×, 3× 512w and 512h, but you can select any number as a multiplier and any number for your height or width. Once you've selected a height, Sketch will calculate the appropriate width, and once you select a height, Sketch will calculate the appropriate height. Sketch also allows you to export multiple versions and sizes of the same element or artboard at the same time. I've included a screenshot of the options in Figure 10-4.

Figure 10-4. Export for size, suffix, and format in Sketch

After you've chosen your size and format, Sketch will add the appropriate suffix to the end of your file name after export as well. Xcode will recognize the suffix during the software development process after the images are imported into Xcode.

> **Tip**   Default size and format options are 1× and PNG.

Quick and Dirty

If you are looking for a painless and easy way to immediately export a layer without doing any of the previously described steps, Sketch has you covered there, too. After you've selected the area that you want to export and it shows up in the inspector as a preview, simply drag it onto your desktop for an immediate conversion to the selected format and size. It doesn't get much easier than that.

Exporting Artboards

Exporting artboards will be something that you do if you're handing off assets and need to show how the finished product will look. More often than not, however, you'll be exporting individual assets such as icons and layers. For now, we'll focus on exporting the artboard itself. The process is extremely straightforward. Let's say that we'd like to export the home page of the PhotoBomb app. First, you would select the entire artboard either in the canvas or in the layer list. With that done, click the Make Exportable button in the lower right corner of the Inspector panel. You will see that the size, suffix, and format settings also appear in

the preview pane. For this example, you can leave it as is. The settings there should be 1×
for size, no suffix, and PNG as the desired format. Clicking the Export button again will bring
up a destination window that allows you to select where the final exported file will be saved.
Figure 10-5 shows the screen just before the export. The final export will be a flattened PNG
file in the designated location.

Figure 10-5. *Home page canvas with Inspector highlighted before exporting*

Exporting Individual Assets

Exporting individual assets is a process that you will most likely be engaging in regularly.
The use of icons in design, especially for iOS is extensive. So, it is important to understand
how to export them for iOS development. Slices can be created and stored as members
of a group folder for easy organization. As you already know, a slice is created by selecting
Slice from the Insert menu drop-down. So say for instance that I am trying to create a slice
of the Start icon in the tab bar. I would create a slice around it. Sketch will intuitively create a
preview of the slice. Once it is adjusted for size, I can select the various versions of the icon
that I need to create for various resolutions as shown in Figure 10-6 and then export all three
icons as an appropriately sized PNG file. Only the slice that is presented in the preview will
be exported.

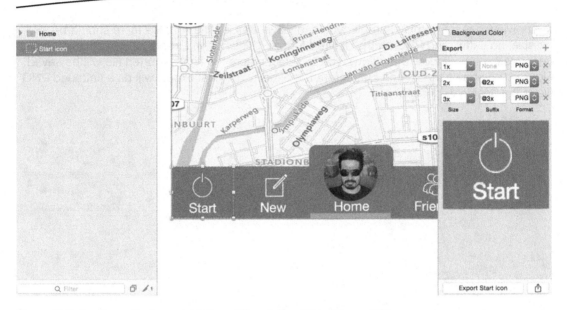

Figure 10-6. Creating a slice for export in three different sizes, @1×, @2×, and @3×

Your slices must be precise, however, as the slice option will slice exactly what is selected within the window. You can always use the inspector to see what part of your image is being selected and subsequently exported.

Creating a Folder for Your Assets

Exporting assets can be a messy job and yet, just like organizing and naming your layers, it's important. So is organizing your assets, especially when you are handing them off to a developer. I try to keep my layers titled intuitively and try to export to folders where a developer can find everything they need. Sketch makes this process easy, too.

Sketch offers a handy feature. By changing the name of your layer and adding a forward slash, Sketch will create a folder with your asset in it. The convention is that whatever is before the forward slash is the name of the folder and whatever is after will be the name of your slice or asset. For example, to create a folder called "Button" with an asset or slice inside called "Check Button" in Figure 10-7, I changed the name of the group to "Button/Check Button." Sketch automatically created a folder with the asset inside.

Figure 10-7. *How to name a layer so that Sketch will automatically create a folder for your assets*

Trimming Backgrounds

Sometimes, when you select a slice for export, Sketch will automatically include the background. But most times, we aren't really looking for the background to be exported with the assets. This is the case particularly with some icons and especially buttons. Sketch has an easy way of dealing with unwanted backgrounds when you really only want the asset itself. Here's how it works. Using our PhotoBomb capture page as an example, let's say that we only want to select the button on this page used to take the actual photograph. As explained previously, you would select the asset. But, when the preview appears in the Inspector as shown in Figure 10-8, we can see that the background image has been included.

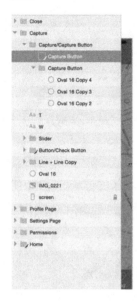

Figure 10-8. *Sometimes Sketch will select a background image for export along with the selected asset*

Since we don't want the background to be exported, we select the check boxes above the preview that allow us to "Export Group Contents Only." This tells Sketch that we aren't interested in background and only selects and exports the asset we want. The resulting exported PNG file is shown in Figure 10-9.

Figure 10-9. *Final exported PNG without the background image*

There you have it. You now have all of the knowledge that you need to export all of your assets in an easy and organized fashion for development.

Summary

With your assets exported and handoff complete, you may still need to check in during the development process to answer questions and do spot creative checks. So far in this book, we've outlined most of the design tasks by using the Sketch program to show you what Sketch can do as a design program. However, there is a vibrant community of developers creating plug-ins that extend Sketch's capabilities. We'll discuss some of those in the next chapter.

Sketch Resources

In this section of the book, we will cover resources from the every growing Sketch community that have been created to make designing with Sketch even easier. This is truly one of the great things about Sketch. The community has rallied around the program, encouraged by Bohemian Coding, and there are now lots of great plug-ins that you can add to increase Sketch's capabilities and improve your workflow. I'll attempt to add as many of them as I am aware of here.

Plug-ins

Plug-ins are great add-ons that expand the capabilities of Sketch. They are created by developers who are interested in expanding the capabilities of Sketch. If you are interested in writing your own plug-ins, you can find some resources and documentation on the Bohemian Coding site.

Installing Plug-ins

If you are searching the Web and come across a plug-in that you think you want to install, here's how to get the plug-in working in Sketch:

1. Download the plug-in and open the file. Usually the files are in a compressed folder.

2. Once you have opened this folder, open Sketch and navigate to the plug-in menu in the toolbar as shown in Figure 11-1 and select "Reveal Plugins Folder." Sketch will automatically open a new window.

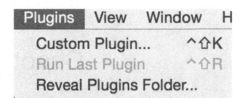

Figure 11-1. *The plug-in drop-down window from the Sketch menu*

3. Drag the Sketch file into the plug-in folder.

4. Your plug-in should now be installed.

Sketch Toolbox

Arguably, the first plug-in you will want to install is Sketch Toolbox. It's like a browser that lists lots of plug-ins available for Sketch. In it, you will find a selection of awesome plug-ins that you can install right from this one plug-in. It is highly recommended to be the first plug-in that you install. To download this plug-in, you can go directly to the website http://www. sketchtoolbox.com, do a search on Google, or download directly from GitHub. I'll walk you through installing the plug-in first from the website. The Sketch Toolbox website is shown in Figure 11-2.

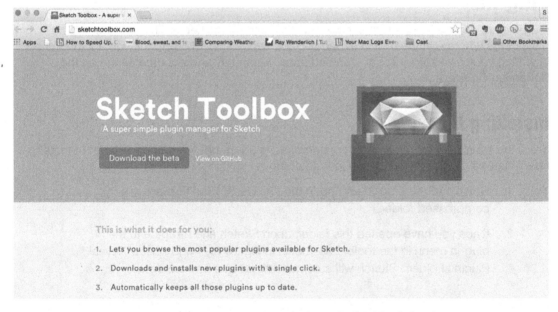

Figure 11-2. *The Sketch Toolbox website. You can download the Sketch Toolbox plug-in from here*

After clicking "Download the beta" button on the site, your download will automatically begin. You can install this application as you would any other Mac OS application, by unzipping and dragging it into your Applications folder.

Tip   Your Mac OS settings may need to be changed to allow applications from developers other than Apple to be installed on your computer.

Once you've installed Sketch Toolbox, you can open it. You will see a scrollable window with a listing of the plug-ins available for installation. Sketch Toolbox allows you to install all plug-ins directly from this interface. This is a much simpler way to install plug-ins. If you choose to install plug-ins directly from GitHub, you will need to follow the directions provided previously. Now, let's go through the process of installing an app via the Sketch Toolbox. Figure 11-3 is a screenshot of the Sketch Toolbox interface.

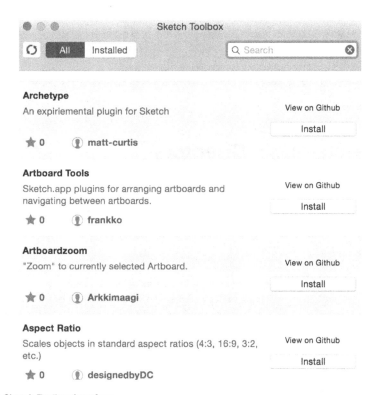

Figure 11-3. *The Sketch Toolbox interface*

As you can see, it is fairly simple. Plug-ins are listed in order alphabetically and there is a brief description of what it does along with the name of the developer. You can choose to install the plug-in by clicking the "Install" button on the interface or can also view the plug-in on GitHub. If you click "View on Github" it will open a new browser window with the plug-in's page on GitHub. For your view, you can also toggle between all available plug-ins or only installed plug-ins.

You are now ready, install all of your plug-ins for Sketch!

> **Tip**   Sketch Toolbox is in beta so might be buggy. Report bugs if you find them to help make the product better.

GitHub

GitHub is a great resource for finding Sketch plug-ins. A Google search for "github sketch plug-ins" will bring up a link to Sketch Plugins (see Figure 11-4). There, you will find a link to all of the Sketch plug-ins available on the GitHub repo.

Figure 11-4. A screenshot of the Sketch Plugin Directory on GitHub, a great resource for Sketch plug-ins

My Favorite Plug-ins

The following is a list of some of my favorite plug-ins that I use in my design workflow.

Content Generator: Content Generator for Sketch lets you generate avatars, names, photos, and text for any design you create.

Sketch Icon Stamper: Automates the process of creating multiple and varied icons in different sizes.

Day Player: Add placeholder images from a variety of sources.

Duplicator: Displays objects, shapes, and elements quickly by duplicating them into grids and lists.

AEiconizer: Lets you generate all of the necessary sizes for your iOS icons.

Sketch Measure: Lets you provide measurements and specs for handing off to developers.

Sketch Squares: Fill your layers or squares with photos from Instagram.

Sketch Export Assets: Resizes and adds metadata to files exported for iOS and other platforms.

Sketch Style Inventory: Review, import, and export your styles.

Sketch to Xcode assets catalog: Exports assets for iOS from Sketch into Xcode assets catalog.

Artboard-Specific Plug-ins

The following plug-ins are for working with artboards in Sketch.

Marvel Sketch: Export your artboards directly into your Marvel prototypes.

Sketch Arrange Artboards: Lays all of your artboards in a grid with a user-specified number of rows.

ArtboardZoom: Easily zoom into the currently selected artboard of a currently selected object.

Sketch Mate: Lets you automatically resize your artboard to fit to layers and content.

Other Resources

Here are links to some great Sketch resources on the Web. This list is by no means complete, as there are great and talented people adding Sketch resources all the time. This is simply my attempt to share some of my favorites.

Websites

Bohemian Coding Sketch Community: `http://bohemiancoding.com/sketch/community/`

The official Bohemian Coding Sketch community.

Sketchapp.tv: `http://sketchapp.tv/`

Video tutorials on Sketch.

SketchLand: http://sketch.land/

Index of Sketch plug-ins.

Sketch App Sources: http://www.sketchappsources.com/

Catalog of free resources for Sketch. Both Web and app development.

Sketch Tricks: http://sketchtricks.com/

A great collection of articles and links on Sketch.

Groups

Sketch Facebook Group: https://www.facebook.com/groups/sketchformac/

Sketch Talk Forum: http://sketchtalk.io/

Sketch on Reddit: https://www.reddit.com/r/sketchapp/

Sketch Collection on Medium: https://medium.com/sketch-app/

Design & Code Facebook Group: https://www.facebook.com/groups/designcode/

SketchDesign.io Facebook Group: https://www.facebook.com/groups/sketchdesignio/

Apps That Integrate with Sketch

Avocode.com: Export and share from Photoshop and Sketch.

Origami: http://facebook.github.io/origami/

Design Prototyping Tools

Invision: http://www.invisionapp.com/

Prototyping and workflow collaboration tool.

Wake: https://wake.io/

Collaborative design tool.

Zeplin: https://zeplin.io/

Lets you generate style guides automatically.

Flinto: https://www.flinto.com/

Design Prototyping tool for Mac.

Marvel: https://marvelapp.com/

Mobile and Web prototyping.

I hope that you find these websites helpful on your design journey.

Summary

The plug-ins mentioned in this chapter are meant to help to speed up your workflow and to assist you with the overall process of designing your app. The plug-ins aren't mandatory, but they are a big part of the growing Sketch community and, as such, are meant to enhance your use of Sketch.

Now that you've come to the end of the book and your design lesson, feel free to join the community, meet other designers, and contribute.

Index

Get the eBook for only $5!

Why limit yourself?

Now you can take the weightless companion with you wherever you go and access your content on your PC, phone, tablet, or reader.

Since you've purchased this print book, we're happy to offer you the eBook in all 3 formats for just $5.

Convenient and fully searchable, the PDF version enables you to easily find and copy code—or perform examples by quickly toggling between instructions and applications. The MOBI format is ideal for your Kindle, while the ePUB can be utilized on a variety of mobile devices.

To learn more, go to www.apress.com/companion or contact support@apress.com.

Apress®
THE EXPERT'S VOICE™

Printed in the United States
By Bookmasters